Britain: Policy and Practice in Continuing Education

Peter Jarvis, *Editor*
University of Surrey

NEW DIRECTIONS FOR CONTINUING EDUCATION
GORDON G. DARKENWALD, *Editor-in-Chief*
Rutgers University

ALAN B. KNOX, *Consulting Editor*
University of Wisconsin

Number 40, Winter 1988

Paperback sourcebooks in
The Jossey-Bass Higher Education Series

Jossey-Bass Inc., Publishers
San Francisco • London

Peter Jarvis (ed.).
Britain: Policy and Practice in Continuing Education.
New Directions for Continuing Education, no. 40.
San Francisco: Jossey-Bass, 1988.

New Directions for Continuing Education
Gordon G. Darkenwald, *Editor-in-Chief*
Alan B. Knox, *Consulting Editor*

Copyright © 1988 by Jossey-Bass Inc., Publishers
and
Jossey-Bass Limited

Copyright under International, Pan American, and Universal Copyright Conventions. All rights reserved. No part of this issue may be reproduced in any form—except for brief quotation (not to exceed 500 words) in a review or professional work—without permission in writing from the publishers.

New Directions for Continuing Education is published quarterly by Jossey-Bass Inc., Publishers (publication number USPS 493-930). Second-class postage paid at San Francisco, California, and at additional mailing offices. POSTMASTER: Send address changes to Jossey-Bass Inc., Publishers, 350 Sansome Street, San Francisco, California 94104.

Editorial correspondence should be sent to the Editor-in-Chief, Gordon G. Darkenwald, Graduate School of Education, Rutgers University, 10 Seminary Place, New Brunswick, New Jersey 08903.

Library of Congress Catalog Card Number LC 85-644750
International Standard Serial Number ISSN 0195-2242
International Standard Book Number ISBN 1-55542-881-9

Cover art by WILLI BAUM
Manufactured in the United States of America. Printed on acid-free paper.

Ordering Information

The paperback sourcebooks listed below are published quarterly and can be ordered either by subscription or single copy.

Subscriptions cost $52.00 per year for institutions, agencies, and libraries. Individuals can subscribe at the special rate of $39.00 per year *if payment is by personal check*. (Note that the full rate of $52.00 applies if payment is by institutional check, even if the subscription is designated for an individual.) Standing orders are accepted.

Single copies are available at $12.95 when payment accompanies order. (California, New Jersey, New York, and Washington, D.C., residents please include appropriate sales tax.) For billed orders, cost per copy is $12.95 plus postage and handling.

Substantial discounts are offered to organizations and individuals wishing to purchase bulk quantities of Jossey-Bass sourcebooks. Please inquire.

Please note that these prices are for the calendar year 1988 and are subject to change without notice. Also, some titles may be out of print and therefore not available for sale.

To ensure correct and prompt delivery, all orders must give either the *name of an individual* or an *official purchase order number*. Please submit your order as follows:

Subscriptions: specify series and year subscription is to begin.
Single Copies: specify sourcebook code (such as, CE1) and first two words of title.

Mail orders for United States and Possessions, Australia, New Zealand, Canada, Latin America, and Japan to:
Jossey-Bass Inc., Publishers
350 Sansome Street
San Francisco, California 94104

Mail orders for all other parts of the world to:
Jossey-Bass Limited
28 Banner Street
London EC1Y 8QE

New Directions for Continuing Education Series
Gordon G. Darkenwald, *Editor-in-Chief*
Alan B. Knox, *Consulting Editor*

CE1 *Enhancing Proficiencies of Continuing Educators,* Alan B. Knox
CE2 *Programming for Adults Facing Mid-Life Change,* Alan B. Knox
CE3 *Assessing the Impact of Continuing Education,* Alan B. Knox

CE4   *Attracting Able Instructors of Adults*, M. Alan Brown, Harlan G. Copeland
CE5   *Providing Continuing Education by Media and Technology*, Martin N. Chamberlain
CE6   *Teaching Adults Effectively*, Alan B. Knox
CE7   *Assessing Educational Needs of Adults*, Floyd C. Pennington
CE8   *Reaching Hard-to-Reach Adults*, Gordon G. Darkenwald, Gordon A. Larson
CE9   *Strengthening Internal Support for Continuing Education*, James C. Votruba
CE10 *Advising and Counseling Adult Learners*, Frank R. DiSilvestro
CE11 *Continuing Education for Community Leadership*, Harold W. Stubblefield
CE12 *Attracting External Funds for Continuing Education*, John H. Buskey
CE13 *Leadership Strategies for Meeting New Challenges*, Alan B. Knox
CE14 *Programs for Older Adults*, Morris A. Okun
CE15 *Linking Philosophy and Practice*, Sharan B. Merriam
CE16 *Creative Financing and Budgeting*, Travis Shipp
CE17 *Materials for Teaching Adults: Selection, Development, and Use*, John P. Wilson
CE18 *Strengthening Connections Between Education and Performance*, Stanley M. Grabowski
CE19 *Helping Adults Learn How to Learn*, Robert M. Smith
CE20 *Educational Outreach to Select Adult Populations*, Carol E. Kasworm
CE21 *Meeting Educational Needs of Young Adults*, Gordon G. Darkenwald, Alan B. Knox
CE22 *Designing and Implementing Effective Workshops*, Thomas J. Sork
CE23 *Realizing the Potential of Interorganizational Cooperation*, Hal Beder
CE24 *Evaluation for Program Improvement*, David Deshler
CE25 *Self-Directed Learning: From Theory to Practice*, Stephen Brookfield
CE26 *Involving Adults in the Educational Process*, Sandra H. Rosenblum
CE27 *Problems and Prospects in Continuing Professional Education*, Ronald M. Cervero, Craig L. Scanlan
CE28 *Improving Conference Design and Outcomes*, Paul J. Ilsley
CE29 *Personal Computers and the Adult Learner*, Barry Heermann
CE30 *Experiential and Simulation Techniques for Teaching Adults*, Linda H. Lewis
CE31 *Marketing Continuing Education*, Hal Beder
CE32 *Issues in Adult Career Counseling*, Juliet V. Miller, Mary Lynne Musgrove
CE33 *Responding to the Educational Needs of Today's Workplace*, Ivan Charner, Catherine A. Rolzinski
CE34 *Technologies for Learning Outside the Classroom*, John A. Niemi, Dennis D. Gooler
CE35 *Competitive Strategies for Continuing Education*, Clifford Baden
CE36 *Continuing Education in the Year 2000*, Ralph G. Brockett
CE37 *China: Lessons from Practice*, Wang Maorong, Lin Weihua, Sun Shilu, Fang Jing
CE38 *Enhancing Staff Development in Diverse Settings*, Victoria J. Marsick
CE39 *Addressing the Needs of Returning Women*, Linda H. Lewis

Contents

Editor's Notes 1
Peter Jarvis

1. A Contextual Framework for Continuing Education 3
Peter Jarvis
The provision of adult education in the United Kingdom is discussed, as is the meaning of the term *continuing education*.

2. Continuing Education and Social Policy 13
Colin Griffin
This chapter provides an analysis of government policy toward continuing education.

3. Continuing Education in Universities and Polytechnics 23
Frankie Todd
Recent policy decisions have resulted in major changes toward continuing education in higher education, and these changes are fully discussed in this chapter.

4. Continuing Education in Colleges of Further Education 33
Laurie S. Piper
Further education has been affected by government policy, and this chapter examines continuing education in further education institutions.

5. Continuing Education in the Trade Union Movement 45
John Holford
Labor union education has been changed by a variety of political decisions, as this chapter illustrates.

6. Educational Initiatives with the Unemployed 55
Nicholas Walters
Structural unemployment has been great in the United Kingdom, and this has resulted in major changes in educational provision for the unemployed.

7. Developments in Continuing Education in the Professions 65
Linda Welsh
The professions are gradually introducing their own policies about continuing education; this chapter contains a report of a recent survey of the professions in the United Kingdom.

8. Open Learning and Continuing Education 75
Malcolm Tight
Open learning offers a coherent methodology and an adaptable range of techniques for the development of continuing education.

9. The Future of Continuing Education 85
Peter Jarvis
This chapter examines the way that general education for adults has fared in the light of emphasis being placed on continuing professional education.

10. Some Implications for Continuing Education in North America 93
Peter Jarvis
Some implications are discussed that might have relevance to North American continuing education.

Index 99

Editor's Notes

This source book endeavors to present a picture of continuing education as it is in 1988 in the United Kingdom. It is recognized that to cover a whole country and to try to discuss such a diversity of activities must result in those chosen being selective. No attempts are made by the authors to cover their topics in depth; instead, it was thought advisable to try to present as broad an overview as possible. At the same time, it is not just present events that are important, but also the implications of these events for both the study of the field of continuing education in particular and for policy analysis about education in general. Thus, a number of the chapters seek to present theoretical analyses, while others are specifically oriented to one part of the field.

Even now there are omissions from this study, such as adult basic education, that would have enriched it. But space forbade the inclusion of additional areas. Additionally, because the structure of education in the United Kingdom is so different from that in the United States, it might have been useful to have included a more complete picture of that structure. In the following paragraph, a very brief overview is presented that might help readers locate the following chapters within the framework and this is elaborated somewhat in the opening chapter. Chapters Two and Nine explore the relationship between the educational provision and national policies, which are clearly related to issues of educational structure.

In the United Kingdom, the government, through the local education authorities, is the main provider of education from school (commencing at five years of age) until age sixteen (end of compulsory schooling) or until children leave school to enter work or further higher education. Further education, discussed in Chapter Four by Piper, is also administered by the local education authorities and commences at sixteen years of age for those who have left school and enrolled in postsecondary education. Further education has traditionally served the young adults who have not stayed at school, but who wish to enter higher education or be prepared for skilled employment. However, in recent years it has expanded its role considerably into the field of continuing education.

Higher education in the United Kingdom—university, polytechnic, and institutes of higher education—has traditionally been full-time for the eighteen-year-plus age group. Recently, however, it has been forced to look at continuing education, as Chapters Three and Six by Todd and Walters show. Adult education for leisure has traditionally been nonvocational and non-award-bearing, but with the formation of

1

the Open University (see Chapter Eight by Tight), this has changed in part. However, the non-award-bearing leisure courses that have been provided by the universities, local education authorities, and the Workers' Educational Association have been made to be more self-supporting (see Chapter Nine). Traditionally, the Workers' Education Association, a government-supported voluntary education, has worked with the trade unions (see Chapter Five by Holford). While industry and commerce have both been a client of the education institution, they have also provided their own continuing education, as Chapter Seven by Walsh demonstrates.

Overall, this study is about the United Kingdom but the final chapter does seek to relate some of the issues of this discussion to the United States, since one of the reasons for international study is to create lessons to be drawn about the provision of continuing education in individual countries.

Peter Jarvis
Editor

Peter Jarvis, senior lecturer in the education of adults, University of Surrey, is coeditor of the International Journal of Lifelong Education *and the author of numerous books and articles, some written from a sociological perspective.*

This chapter outlines the provision of adult education in the United Kingdom and enters briefly into a conceptual discussion about the meaning of the term.

A Contextual Framework for Continuing Education

Peter Jarvis

Finding one's way around adult education in any country is difficult because postcompulsory education the world over has no rigid framework, a point made by Malcolm Knowles (1977) in his discussion of the nature of adult education. Hence this chapter seeks first to guide readers through the semantic and conceptual undergrowth surrounding the term, then to introduce them to the complexity of adult education in the United Kingdom, and, finally, to locate the following chapters within the framework provided by this introduction.

A Definition of Continuing Education

The concept of continuing education is one around which there has been considerable debate in the United Kingdom, although it is not the intention of this chapter to try to unravel all its complexity. However, a brief look into the area will help provide a backdrop to the following chapters.

In 1973 a major report on adult education was published in United Kingdom, which became known as the Russell Report (Russell, 1973), in which it was recommended that a Development Council for Adult Education be established for England and Wales. However, no immediate response was forthcoming from the government. In 1976 the Open University published its report on continuing education, known after its chairman, Sir Peter Venables, as the Venables Report (Venables, 1976). The report called for a National Council for Adult and Continuing Education. Eventually, the government of the time responded to these calls, not by establishing a national council, but by creating an Advisory Council for Adult and Continuing Education in 1977. That council was initially given a remit for three years, but it was extended by the Conservative government, which had subsequently come to power, for a further three years. Thus, the term *continuing education* had arrived on the educational scene. Yet there was no agreed definition of the term.

The Venables Committee (1976, p. 19) defined continuing education as "all learning opportunities which are taken up after full-time compulsory schooling has ceased." This definition did not pass uncriticized. MacIntosh (1979, p. 3), for instance, claimed that continuing education only began after initial education had been completed, while the Advisory Council report on continuing education (1982, p. 1) merely stated that adults should be given continued educational opportunities throughout their lives. By 1984, when there was yet another report on continuing education, this time by the University Grants Commission (1984), the term had really come to prominence. It embraced all educational and training opportunities, whether in work or leisure, throughout adult life. This very broad definition is the one that is adopted here. However, it will be seen in the remainder of this volume that while it has been used in much of the official literature, there is still a sense that there is a differentiation between forms of education for adults. However, in order to clarify the following pages, it is now necessary to give a brief overview of the provision of continuing education in the United Kingdom.

Continuing Education in England and Wales

This chapter looks only at England and Wales, specifically, since some of the state provision of continuing education in Scotland is slightly different. To provide this overview, this section is divided into four subsections: the first deals with local government provision; the second, with the universities; the third looks briefly at other providers; and in the last, continuing education in the professions, industry, and commerce is discussed.

Local Government Provision. It will be seen from the above discussion that prior to the 1970s, the term *adult education* was more prevalent than it is at present. However, there is another term that has currency in the United Kingdom, namely, *further education*. Traditionally, further education has referred to all education provided by local education authorities, that is, local government, for those who have left school, which has also included adult education. Indeed, this has been a statutory duty of the local authority since the 1944 Education Act, which specified:

> Section 4.1: Subject as hereinafter provided, it shall be the duty of every local education authority to secure the provision for their area of adequate facilities for further education, that is to say:
>   a. full-time and part-time education for persons over compulsory school age; and
>   b. leisure time occupation, in such organized cultural training and recreative activities as are suited to their requirements, for any persons over compulsory school age who are able and willing to profit by the facilities provided for that purpose [cited in Stock, 1982, p. 12].

From the terms of the 1944 Education Act, it would appear that the task of describing continuing education in the United Kingdom is relatively uncomplicated, but this is because the act, which is currently being replaced by new educational legislation, is of historical significance and really concerned only with local government provision. In reality, the provision is much more complex, and the following few paragraphs only outline a little of it; a fuller account may be found in Jarvis (1983, p. 251–279).

This legislation is clearly mainly about liberal adult education, but then it must be remembered that in 1944, the country was still engaged in a war, so that the legislation reflects the forward-looking thinking of people concerned for the type of provision to be made for adults after the war was over. Clearly, the local government authorities were being expected to do something that had never been undertaken in such a major way before: to provide further educational opportunities for all adults in their areas. This emerged in the 1950s and 1960s in four quite different forms: higher education, further education, adult education, and community colleges. While each can be described separately, there is considerable overlap between these forms.

Higher education in this case does not include the universities. First, because they have never been under the control of local government; second, because the norm has been that students would go to university full time directly from school, there is a sense in which universities have always, until very recently, been treated as separate from adult and continuing education. It was in the 1960s that the polytechnics were established, and it was generally recognized that they would provide both vocational and advanced courses in general education for adults. In the 1970s the teacher training colleges were forced to diversify, and some of these merged with polytechnics and universities. Others became independent colleges of higher education, and they also offered advanced courses in vocational and general education. For a variety of reasons, these colleges offered many of their courses to adults. While both the polytechnics and the colleges of higher education have to some extent tried to be like the universities, they also have, until recently, developed many more initiatives in continuing education than the universities. The one major exception to this is the Open University, which started offering its courses to adults at the start of the 1970s and has become the largest provider of continuing education in the United Kingdom.

Less-advanced work relating to the education of adults has been undertaken by colleges of further education. The distinction between further and advanced education often appears blurred, but it is generally assumed that for educational work above the level of the General Certificate of Education (advanced level), an examination taken by school leavers seeking a university placement is required. Colleges of further education have traditionally offered a mixture of lower-status vocational training and lower-level education for adults, but as they have extended their work, these colleges now often offer a great deal of advanced work as well, so that the differentiation between higher and further education remains rather problematic, in institutional terms.

Much of the work of colleges of further education has been of a vocational nature, and a significant development in recent years has been that many of these courses have no longer been funded or controlled by the college or local government. The Manpower Services Commission (recently renamed the Training Commission, and subsequently, the Training Agency), established by the Department of Trade and Industry as a government initiative, has sponsored relevant education and training to young adults in these colleges throughout the country. It has provided funds to the colleges for the provision of these courses in their area. Hence, some of the local control has been removed from these colleges, and even from the Department of Education and Science, as Manpower Services Commission courses are more centrally controlled.

Some local education authorities have also established within the colleges of further education a separate department responsible solely for liberal adult education in their area, whereas other authorities have established separate adult education institutes. This provision differs from area to area, so that it is difficult to provide a straightforward picture of what is occurring in the United Kingdom.

However, the adult education institutes have tended to be smaller organizations, having a smaller full-time staff which has organized adult education throughout the area. They have employed many part-time staff, used school rooms in the evenings, and have generally sought to provide a full program in the locality. While these institutions have tried extremely hard to provide a varied program that would cater to the needs of all adults in the area, it has generally been agreed that they have been most successful with the middle-class populations (Westwood, 1980).

The further education colleges in the United Kingdom are in some ways very similar to the community colleges in the United States, whereas the community colleges in the United Kingdom were much more the result of the vision of one man, Henry Morris, who in the 1930s tried to get local education authorities to establish colleges in small towns and villages, hoping the colleges could become community centers, offering not only education but also other health and cultural activities. These types of colleges have been established in a few places throughout the United Kingdom, but they are comparatively rare, and often when the term *community college* is now used in the United Kingdom, it refers to a school that is seeking to work with adults as well as children by offering a small program for adults.

The Universities. Apart from the Open University, the traditional universities, which have never been under the control of local government, have not organized degree-level programs especially for adults, although most of them have had special provisions for mature students to join the normal degree program for the full-time students. Yet they have not been inactive in the provision of extramural education. As early as 1867, James Stuart of the University of Cambridge delivered a course of lectures for the North of England Council for Providing Higher Education for Women, and this is generally regarded as the start of the university extension movement in England. The movement was actually formerly sanctioned by the University in 1873, and eventually, the national government granted "responsible body" status to twenty-five universities; that is, the universities were given special financial grants and the responsibility to organize liberal adult education programs within their special locality. This special funding is in the process of being withdrawn by current legislation, although it is anticipated that most universities will offer an extension program, even though it will be forced to assume a different form than it has had previously.

Apart from this "responsible body" work, the University of London has traditionally been the only one of the established universities in England and Wales that has catered to adults. First, Birkbeck College is a constituent college of the university, and its focus has always been part-time education for adults. Second, Birkbeck has been the only university to organize a special external degree program for adults, which has been very successful over the years. Now, a number of universities offering part-time degree programs for adults and at least two other universities—the Open University and the University of Surrey—are providing distance education courses to master's degree level.

More recently, the universities and the polytechnics have been encouraged to focus some of their work in the area of continuing professional education, with the enticement of financial assistance for approved projects from the Department of Education and Science. These financial grants are regarded as "pump priming" rather than permanent assistance and usually are for a very limited period of time. However, these efforts reflect a part of the change in the British system of higher education and part-time study for adults—namely, that such education is becoming much more accepted and more widely practiced, and a whole new educational movement of increased access to educational opportunities is coming to the fore.

Other Providers. Apart from local government and university provision, there has been a wide variety of other providers; three types are briefly mentioned here: voluntary organizations, residential colleges, and independent educational organizations.

Among the most significant voluntary organizations providing education for adults is the Workers' Educational Association (WEA). Founded in 1903 by Albert Mansbridge, although it did not assume its name until 1905, the WEA also has "responsible body" status from the Department of Education and Science. It is a national body, divided into seventeen districts in England and Wales, three in Scotland, and one in Northern Ireland. Within each district there are branches in most towns and cities; each branch is autonomous so that members' interests are paramount in the construction of the program. However, the WEA was founded to assist the working people of Britain, and the Russell Report (Russell, 1973) stressed that the association should work with industry and the disadvantaged.

It would be difficult to mention all of the other voluntary organizations that have played a significant part in the provision of continuing education, but there are two major women's organizations: the Women's Institute and the Townswomen's Guilds. Both of these are national institutions and have provided a wide variety of educational activities for adult women; the former has been especially significant in its work in rural England. Finally, and in common with most countries in the world, the churches have always played a major role in the provision of education for adults, and while their educational activities among adults is rarely as formalized as it is in America, the churches have contributed a great deal to the development of adult education in Britain.

A feature of continuing education in Britain has been the residential colleges, founded on similar lines to the residential folk high schools in Denmark. There are basically two types of residential college: those that provide courses for an academic year or longer and those that organize short-course provision only. There are currently nine long-term colleges, Ruskin College being the oldest, while Northern College was founded only in 1977. All the colleges offer courses to adults of both sexes, with the exception of Hillcroft College, which is for female students only.

Two of the colleges have a religious foundation, Plater being a college of the Church of Rome, while Woodbrooke is organized by the Society of Friends. Many students attending these colleges receive grant aid from the state. Apart from these colleges, there are about fifty short-term colleges that organize short-term courses, both work and leisure related. Often the work-related courses are organized in relation to specific companies and their training needs. These colleges often employ a full-time principal or warden, who then employs specialist teachers on a part-time basis to provide specific input.

Finally, in this subsection, the independent providers must be noted. There are a huge variety of organizations offering all forms of education: correspondence colleges, conference centers, independent adult education centers in local towns, commercial schools, language schools, and so on. The language schools are at the present time flourishing because of the significance of English as an international language.

Continuing Professional Education. It was noted above that the professions, industry, and commerce often use the independent short-term residential colleges for some of their own courses of training. However, they also relate with the universities and polytechnics in some of their advanced work, but also most of the major occupations and many of the leading employers have their own colleges. Until recently, there has been no way that these colleges could award educational qualifications that would have credit on other courses. However, recently a Credit Accumulation and Transfer Scheme has been devised in the United Kingdom by the Council for National Academic Awards, which is going to allow this to happen. It is anticipated that this scheme will have quite far-reaching effects on continuing education in the United Kingdom over the coming years.

Traditionally, the professions have all sought to locate their initial preparation in institutions of higher education because of the status this gives and also because recruits can gain both a professional and an academic qualification. This situation will no doubt continue unchanged, and those lower-status professions, such as nursing, will continue to strive for access to these institutions. The extent to which they will seek to locate their continuing professional education in such institutions if they can gain academic credit for their own courses is much more problematic.

Conclusion

It will be seen from the above description that the provision of continuing education in Britain is a complex phenomenon that cannot be adequately described in a few paragraphs. However, readers will have some idea of the situation so that the following chapters can be located within the broader framework.

On a few occasions in this chapter, it has been noted that there has been statutory legislation about continuing education in the United Kingdom and that there is, at the time of writing, additional legislation under consideration. Chapter Two seeks to examine government policy and the effects that such legislation is having on continuing education generally. In the same way, Chapter Nine examines the effects of government policy on the local education authority provision, which was discussed above.

Chapter Three examines the ways that higher education is changing in the light of government initiatives to direct some of its energies toward business and industry; Chapter Four does precisely the same for the colleges of further education. Chapter Seven concentrates on what is occurring in the professions, business, and industry, without special reference to educational institutions.

The role of the Workers' Educational Association was discussed quite fully above, and this organization has traditionally been one of the major providers of educational work with the labor unions. Chapter Five examines the trends that are occurring in this field. By contrast, Chapter Six looks at some of the outreach work that has been occurring in the United Kingdom with the unemployed.

Education for adults has been changing rapidly over the past few years, which is evident from many of the points made above. Hence, the theme of Chapter Eight is an exploration of one of the major changes that has occurred. Finally, Chapter Ten outlines a few aspects that might be relevant to North American continuing education.

References

Advisory Council on Adult and Continuing Education (ACACE). *Continuing Education: From Policies to Practice.* Leicester, UK: ACACE, 1982.

Jarvis, P. *Adult and Continuing Education: Theory and Practice.* London: Croom Helm, 1983.

Knowles, M. S. *The Adult Education Movement in the United States.* New York: Krieger, 1977.

MacIntosh, N. "To Make Continuing Education a Reality." *Oxford Review of Education,* 1979, 5 (2), 1-15.

Russell, L. *Adult Education: A Plan for Development.* London: Her Majesty's Stationery Office, 1973.

Stock, A. *Adult Education in the United Kingdom.* Leicester, UK: National Institute of Adult Continuing Education, 1982.

University Grants Commission (UGC). *Report of the Continuing Education Working Party.* London: UGC, 1984.

Venables, P. *Report of the Committee on Continuing Education.* Milton Keynes, UK: Open University, 1976.

Westwood, S. "Adult Education and the Sociology of Adult Education: An Exploration." In J. Thompson (ed.), *Adult Education for a Change*. London: Heinemann, 1980.

Peter Jarvis is senior lecturer in the education of adults, University of Surrey, Guildford, Surrey, UK.

The dismantling of social welfare functions has reduced liberal adult education to a residual role, while continuing education increasingly reflects a manpower-planning model of social policy addressed to the needs of the economy.

Continuing Education and Social Policy

Colin Griffin

In Britain today, Margaret Thatcher's third consecutive Conservative administration is intent on a radical change of direction in economic, social, and political policy. The major thrust of her policy is now toward the dismantling of the welfare state in favor of greater individual self-help, more individual responsibility, and the free play of market forces in the economy. But what is, or was, the welfare state in Britain? And what has its passing to do with recent developments in adult and continuing education in the country? The aim of this chapter is to establish the relevance of social policy analysis for our understanding of these developments and, in particular, to locate them in the context of Thatcher's social and economic policy revolution. This means thinking about adult and continuing education in Britain as a form of social welfare policy whose fate is very closely tied to that of the welfare state itself.

The Welfare State

It is important to understand what the welfare state amounted to in Britain. In the first place, public welfare provision, albeit of a limited kind, far outdates the advent of the modern state itself: it can be traced back, perhaps, to feudalism.

The legislative program that established welfare in its modern form is certainly associated with the Labour administration elected in 1945 rather than to one led by the war leader Winston Churchill. And yet the program (for extensive nationalization of industry, public health care, universal secondary education, housing, social security, and so on) had been hammered out during the war years of political coalition and consensus. Conservatives, liberals, and socialists were all responsible for aspects of the modern welfare state, although that is not to say it was wholly unopposed or undisputed. It was not so much socialism as a form of progressive liberalism that underpinned the ideology of welfare (George and Wilding, 1976).

Analyzing Welfare

Certainly, academic analysis of what has come to be described as "welfare capitalism" rather than the "welfare state" has, since the 1950s, constituted a distinct social science discipline in Britain. In addition to a substantial body of empirical research into the workings and effectiveness of welfare policy, a range of analytic policy models has been devised to facilitate comparative and historical study (Pinker, 1971; Titmuss, 1974). These are the models that, it is suggested, enable us to conceptualize adult and continuing education in terms of social welfare policy.

The history and structure of adult education provision in Britain shares many characteristics with other aspects and forms of social welfare. It owed its origins not to the state but to popular social movements around religion and politics in the nineteenth century, particularly as these affected the urban, working-class population. Adult education constitutes a "mixed economy" of provision, in that the state, voluntary organizations, and the private market all continue to play a part. In fact, the role of the state has traditionally been indirect and ambiguous, and the legal status of adult education is only discretionary. Policy has originated in those professional bodies and committees that over the years have advised and reported to a succession of governments. Traditionally, too, the ruling ideology of adult education has been liberal-progressive rather than socialist.

In reconciling individual aspirations with social justice, and the role of the state and its agencies with a more libertarian approach, adult education has ideological roots in common with other forms of social welfare derived from progressive liberalism or Fabian socialism. Indeed, the Adult Education Committee (AEC) of the British Ministry of Reconstruction produced a famous report after the World War I in 1919 that expressly linked adult education with the principles of liberal democratic citizenship (Waller, 1956).

Analyzing Adult and Continuing Education

Social policy analysis, which the 1919 report and subsequent policy formulations for adult education directly invite, constitutes a distinctive way of approaching adult education. It focuses adult education as a form of public provision, having many shared characteristics with other social welfare policies. It has, for example, a common discourse of needs, rights, citizenship, social participation, and so on. Policy analysis is distinct from sociological analysis too (Jarvis, 1985), in that its focus is primarily normative and ideological and is concerned with the assumptions underlying decision making, funding, and other principles and values that in the end shape the structure of publicly provided learning opportunities for adults.

In fact, states and governments of many different kinds have never been more interested in promoting forms of adult learning, especially in contexts of rapid economic and social change (Styler, 1984). And despite Thatcher's determination to roll back the boundaries of the state, Britain's education system is in the grip of powerful centralizing tendencies. Many current issues therefore lend themselves to policy analysis: the vocationalism of most continuing education; the stress on postexperience vocational and professional education; and the crisis and near collapse of traditional liberal adult education, largely provided by the local education authorities that fund it by way of local taxation supplemented by money from the central government. There is a financial stringency of the same order that characterizes the National Health Service, local government, or indeed all aspects of what can generally be described as public welfare. There are, of course, some sources of resistance in women's education or community education projects for the unemployed, but increasingly in Britain, adult and, specifically, continuing education are directed toward priorities determined by the state. And it is on this basis that they are publicly funded as objects of social policy, along with other dwindling provisions of the welfare state.

Models of Welfare Policy

Three relevant models of social welfare policy can be derived from the tradition of social policy analysis in Britain: the market, or "residual welfare" model, the liberal-progressive model, and the social control model.

The market model is based simply on the principle derived from classical economics, namely, that intervention in the free market of anything (including adult education as such) will be self-defeating and that state interference into the private realm on whatever grounds is morally and politically destructive. In fact, from Adam Smith to Milton Friedman, there is a remarkable consistency in this model, which advocates the least possible government interference in the voluntary exchange and spontaneous cooperation of the market in goods and services. As a description of tendencies in adult education, the market model poses the sharpest Thatcherite question: Why should any individual subsidize another individual's learning? This has been noticed in particular relation to recreative learning, where it is not self-evident that someone's liberty (to dispose of their own income) should be infringed in order to support the personal growth through learning of someone else.

In theory, liberal adult educators tend to justify redistributive state interference in terms of the democratic virtue and collective benefit of educated, informed, and participative citizens. In practice, the economics of the marketplace have located the burden of payment for liberal and recreative education much more on the consumer, reflecting a Thatcherite but perhaps not unduly cynical view that people who consume liberal adult education probably benefit as individuals and thus should pay the full market price. In short, the market model, increasingly invoked by the government for traditional liberal adult education, assumes that it is not the business of the state to subsidize learning that meets individual needs as such. The task before professional adult educators is therefore to reconstruct individual needs as society's needs, and this has been attempted in various ways such that alternative policy models can be operated to confer social welfare status on adult education provision (Finch, 1984).

In Britain, the major source of transformation of individuals' needs into society's learning needs has involved a liberal-progressive model—the very model that underpins the social policy of welfare capitalism. The development of continuing education in this country reflects such a transformation of individuals' learning needs into the learning needs of society itself and the incorporation by the state and its agencies of liberal adult education into public welfare policy. Whereas the pure form of the market model of social policy is based on the rejection of any principle of distribution other than market forces, the liberal-progressive model squares more with the facts of life in most nonsocialist societies; in practice, the role of the state is to intervene to support the private market and, consequently, to take ever greater control of the education system.

The liberal-progressive case is that sometimes (perhaps not too often) individual freedom can only be secured through state intervention. The welfare state is an example of beneficent intervention in order to secure freedom for individuals who could not secure it for themselves under free market conditions. From a pure market point of view, this model introduces doubtful concepts of equality, which is why it is called liberal-*progressive*, and therefore of the leveling and the threat to individual responsibility that progressivism implies. The model certainly depends for its moral force on certain general principles of freedom, equality, and citizenship without which individual freedom would be only an empty abstraction (Tawney, 1921). In any case, the outcome of applying such a model is that adult education should be subsidized by the state on the grounds of promoting substantive individual freedom, and that therefore those who do not choose to avail themselves of learning opportunities can be legitimately taxed to support the learning of those who do. This is quite contrary to the principles of Adam Smith or Milton Friedman, of course, not least because they would consider that the harm done to the nonlearner (interfering with his right to dispose of his income) outweighed the gain (in personal growth or development) accruing to the learner. But presumably adult educators who adopt a humanistic perspective and who support public provision have nowhere else to go for an argument in favor of it.

Fortunately, perhaps, in a democracy, adult educators do not themselves ultimately determine the funding of adult education by the state or its agents, or state-subsidized voluntary bodies (any diversion of taxpayers' money), even though they properly exercise influence over what proportion of the education budget comes to their sector, usually a very small proportion, indeed, as far as liberal adult education is concerned. Nevertheless, in Britain, the policy issues generated in this liberal-progressive model have finally forced a crucial distinction between adult and continuing education. Adult education, it has become obvious, has been associated mainly with an individualistic, primarily nonvocational, and latterly overwhemlingly recreative kind of provision, particularly in the dominant local education authority sector. The fissure in the liberal-progressive model may be remarked in the publication in 1973 of the Russell Report on nonvocational adult education (Russell, 1973), but its publication coincided with the onset of economic depression and carried little weight with the government of the day. It was a splendid but unpersuasive example of the liberal-progressive social welfare policy model. In other words, it advocated a more systematic and professional adult education service that would address individual learning needs and society's needs, too. In fact, the political mistake was probably to appear to claim that adult education could meet every conceivable human need. There were no priorities except in the sense that everything was a priority, and the needs of individuals and of society were assumed universally to coincide.

Adult and Continuing Education

Even so, it is to the Russell Report that we must look to find an early instance of the emergent distinction between adult and continuing education, a distinction expressed much more in social policy than in educational terms.

In considering individuals' learning needs, the AEC inevitably had to deal with the impact of industrial, technological, and economic change on employment. The concept of continuing education was subsequently developed in these terms, which Titmuss (1958) once described as the industrial performance-achievement model. In other words, a model of adult education as the "handmaiden" of the economy, just as Titmuss and others once saw the welfare state itself as a strategy for integrating society during periods of rapid, dislocating change, serving the interests of capital as Marxists might see it. However, whereas Russell saw adult education itself as an agent of social change, through its mobilization of individual capacities, later models of continuing education rested on the assumption that change is generated in the economy of society and that adult education is a coping, or managing, strategy, one essentially of adaptation on the part of individuals to the requirements and necessities of social and economic change. Government funding and support would thus be attracted to those models of provision that address society's needs even though the rhetoric continues to be organized around individuals' needs. The Open University—which, being more technologically oriented, did succeed in attracting government support—itself contributed significantly to the development of a model of continuing education. In a major report, the case was argued that continuing education has the social benefit of enabling an individual to adapt positively to changing circumstances, to prepare for the new opportunities that such changes may offer, and to become equipped to understand and influence such changes. (Open University, 1976). Perhaps this is a more mutual and dynamic account of the relation between individuals' and society's needs, but essentially the "natural harmony" of interests of the liberal-progressive model is still in evidence.

When therefore the Advisory Council for Adult and Continuing Education (ACACE) was set up in 1977, adult and continuing education had emerged in uneasy relation. Adult education stood for liberal nonvocational provision, whereas continuing education was coming to stand for something rather different. At least, the council produced separate reports on adult, or adult general, education and continuing education (ACACE, 1981, 1982). By far the most important was that on continuing education, which by then had emerged quite explicitly as a manpower-planning strategy of social policy, manifestly addressing issues of individuals' integration into a rapidly changing society in the same way as other social welfare policies. The report represented a marked shift in the direction of society's benefit models of publicly provided adult education in the vocational sphere. Continuing education, as that aspect of organized adult learning that relates to the role of individuals in adapting to the necessities of social and economic change, has since been widely developed, compared with other forms of adult learning provision (Costello and Richardson, 1982; Titmus, 1985). It has been regarded as a major source of salvation for the higher (university and polytechnic) education sector in Britain and is a broad enough idea to encompass the whole spectrum of adult learning, which is likely to reflect a model of individual adaptation to socioeconomic changes.

There is plenty of evidence of an almost universal adoption of the policy models of welfare capitalism—of the liberal-progressive reconciliation of individuals' and society's needs. Generally, the whole idea of change is projected as universal and inevitable and, curiously, not something that could be controlled so as to be adjusted to individual needs should these differ from those of society itself. The overwhelming assumption seems to be that although social change is out of control, individuals are not. But in any case, the model does not permit genuine or irreconcilable conflicts of interest, purpose, or need between individuals and society.

There can be little doubt that many, if not most, adult educators would still hold to models of provision reflecting moral principles of equality of opportunity, or political principles of redistribution of life chances for individuals in society. However, in Britain today, "society's benefit" rationales tend to determine policy. The process of prioritizing "special needs" and of identifying target groups in the population has been taken well beyond Russell by ACACE. In other words, as a form of social welfare policy, adult education in this country is increasingly addressed to problems of the social system or social change. In addition, adult educators, while gaining more control over the discourse of their profession, have effectively lost control of the process of prioritization itself to the state and its agencies, especially in the field of manpower planning. Here the agenda is determined by the Manpower Services Commission (MSC). Of course, it is not possible to separate individuals' from society's needs except at the cost of some abstraction, but, increasingly, individual need is regarded as the need to adapt to new social and economic consequences for employment, or the lack of it. Therefore, it is not only the vocational dimension that marks off continuing education from traditional adult education but the fact that it explicitly embodies a social welfare policy model addressed to the needs of the economy. Adult educators have little choice but to embrace continuing education.

From a Marxist point of view, all social policy models under a welfare capitalist system such as Britain's are concerned with the overriding imperatives of capital itself. In Britain, scholars working in or around this perspective have been occupied in several policy contexts with the rediscovery of a "political economy" analysis of needs (Armstrong, 1983; Leonard, 1984; Phillipson, 1982; Delphy, 1984). Such approaches all reflect a materialist analysis of society in which concepts of class or other forms of social conflict are central. They all imply, in one way or another, that social welfare policies are a form of social control exercised in the interest of capital and in which the state itself is implicated. It follows that adult and continuing education, too, are implicated in social control under the guise of meeting individual needs. However, the development of continuing education in various fields related to the economy and manpower development strategies is hardly a concealed process: the present government has more than once manifested its suspicion that the education system in Britain is not sufficiently addressing itself to the economic needs of society, in which case provision has been taken out of the hands of educators and placed more safely in those of government agencies such as the MSC, which are directly concerned with industry's and government's economic priorities and which are in a position to disburse substantial funds.

Continuing Education and Social Policy

If we consider the major assumptions of, say, the key documents and reports of ACACE, it is not difficult to understand the construction of continuing education as a social policy model nor the construction of a relationship between traditional adult education and continuing education itself. It so happens, because both stem from common liberal-progressive ideological roots, that adult learning theory and continuing education policies lay heavy stress on functional adaptation and integration in individual and social terms. To that extent, it becomes a matter of indifference whether one stresses the individual or society: their purposes are, in effect, one. The needs of individuals are to adapt to the circumstances in which they find themselves. The model of continuing education developed in Britain since the publication of the Russell Report expresses exactly the kind of issues that social policy analysis of adult education addresses:

> The concept of continuing education illustrates directly that of adult education as social policy, in the process whereby the learning or personal growth needs of individuals are categorized in the form of social priorities, professional strategies and target-group populations which, in the last analysis, are addressed to issues of social change [Griffin, 1987, p. 223].

Of course, from an economic point of view, adult learning is problematic in public policy terms: "the fundamental issue for educational policy is to decide and implement public policy on the availability and distribution of *learning* opportunities for adults, whether or not these occur in the context of formal education" (Drake, 1983, p. 3). Social policy analysis of adult and continuing education as a form of welfare provision is based on the assumption that learning opportunities for adults are, in fact, distributed according to criteria determined outside the education system itself: it is left to adult educators to reflect on the nature of adult learning as such, but this is unlikely to influence the distribution of funds to support adult education as social policy. Learning and education are quite different things. The frameworks for developing continuing education are being constructed in a range of professional and educational contexts, as other contributions to this volume show, and although there remain obstacles to its further development, there can be little doubt that continuing education is seen as being in the interests of individuals as employees as well as in that of further and higher education providers. Individual and institutional as well as social and economic needs largely coincide. This is postulated on a policy model of functional adaptation and integration in a fairly deterministic mode. For how in our society could an individual's best interests *not* be served by her or his employability? Or how could an employer's needs *not* be best met by a trained, fulfilled, and well-motivated worker?

Traditional adult education is perhaps postulated on less deterministic assumptions, although, to be fair, it has not necessarily contributed to a more critical approach to the interface of individual and social needs. Much of it remains culturally reproductive and, indeed, soporific: liberal adult education was seldom the powerhouse of intellectual or cultural challenge to incorporation that many defenders of it assert in the face of the inroads of the MSC. Nevertheless, thinking of adult and continuing education in terms of social policy does suggest a distinction in more than merely conceptual or philosophical ways: for whereas adult education traditionally reconciled individual needs with those of society, continuing education seems more concerned with reconciling them to society. Thatcher, in rolling back the state in some of its functions with respect to social welfare, has also rolled back those functions to do with economic policy. Continuing education in Britain, therefore, stands not only for a policy model of education but for a reconceptualization of the whole idea of individual adult learning needs and their incorporation into public policy.

References

Advisory Council for Adult and Continuing Education (ACACE). *Protecting the Future for Adult Education*. Leicester, UK: ACACE, 1981.

Advisory Council for Adult and Continuing Education (ACACE). *Continuing Education: From Policies to Practice*. Leicester, UK: ACACE, 1982.
Armstrong, P. F. "The 'Needs-Meeting' Ideology in Liberal Adult Education." *International Journal of Lifelong Education*, 1983, *1* (4), 293-321.
Costello, N., and Richardson, M. (eds.). *Continuing Education for the Post-Industrial Society*. Milton Keynes, UK: Open University Press, 1982.
Delphy, C. *Close to Home: A Materialistic Analysis of Women's Oppression*. London: Hutchinson, 1984.
Drake, K. *Financing Adult Education and Training*. Manchester, UK: University Department of Adult and Higher Education, 1983.
Finch, G. *Education as Social Policy*. London: Longman, 1984.
George, V., and Wilding, P. *Ideology and Social Welfare*. London: Routledge & Kegan Paul, 1976.
Griffin, C. *Adult Education as Social Policy*. London: Croom Helm, 1987.
Jarvis, P. *The Sociology of Adult and Continuing Education*. London: Croom Helm, 1985.
Leonard, P. *Personality and Ideology*. London: Macmillan, 1984.
Open University. *Report of the Committee on Continuing Education*. Milton Keynes, UK: Open University, 1976.
Phillipson, C. *Capitalism and the Construction of Old Age*. London: Macmillan, 1982.
Pinker, R. *Social Theory and Social Policy*. London: Heinemann, 1971.
Russell, L. *Adult Education: A Plan for Development*. London: Her Majesty's Stationery Office, 1973.
Styler, W. *Adult Education and Political Systems*. Nottingham, UK: University Department of Adult Education, 1984.
Tawney, R. *The Acquisitive Society*. London: Bell, 1921.
Titmus, C. (ed.). *Widening the Field: Continuing Education in Higher Education*. Guildford, UK: Society of Research into Higher Education and NFER/Nelson, 1985.
Titmuss, R. *Essays on the Welfare State*. London: Allen & Unwin, 1958.
Titmuss, R. *Social Policy: An Introduction*. London: Allen & Unwin, 1974.
Waller, R. (ed.). *A Design for Democracy*. London: Max Parrish, 1956.

Colin Griffin is a senior lecturer at Hillcroft College, Sunbiten, Surrey, UK.

Shifts in continuing education suggest major role changes for British universities and polytechnics—but will the potential be achieved, and in what form?

Continuing Education in Universities and Polytechnics

Frankie Todd

In 1977 a British educationalist wrote that "we are in short face to face with the chance of a creative revolution in education" (Burgess, 1977, p. 135). In 1985 the Conservative government's then Secretary of State for Employment claimed that Britain was in the midst of "our own cultural revolution," which in terms of educational provision was producing "an irreversible and historic shift" (Young, 1985). What constitutes a revolution clearly depends on one's starting point. Burgess's vision was based on the principle that "all educational planning and organization should start from the individual adult student" (p. 171). Lord Young's starting points were the requirements of the economy for high caliber manpower (sic) and the need for the greater integration of the education system with industry. These two quotations, only eight years apart in time but light-years apart in terms of educational vision, capture some of the current contradictions in continuing education in the United Kingdom. Not the least of these contradictions is the use of similar terminology and the advocacy of similar educational measures by those pursuing different educational ends.

To understand current policies and provision for continuing education in universities and polytechnics, it is necessary to have some understanding of their differing circumstances and histories.

Routes to Continuing Education

Universities and polytechnics in the United Kingdom come to continuing education via routes that express the differences between them as institutions. Universities have always been autonomous as degree-awarding institutions (the autonomy deriving from royal charters at the time of each university's foundation) and have guarded a tradition of high-level scholarship for its own sake, which can be traced back to their medieval and monastic beginnings. The undergraduate intake of British universities in contemporary times has been primarily in the eighteen- to twenty-one-year-old age group. Adult students have had only three main means of access to university provision: (1) by belonging to a professional or vocational group for which postqualificatory provision has been available—medicine, engineering, or teaching, for instance; (2) by following courses of liberal adult education taught in departments of extramural studies or adult education (some of them ultimately to degree or certificate level but many of them short "leisure" courses); and (3) by gaining mature student matriculation and so progressing on to a full-time degree course. Comparatively small numbers of adults have been able to follow this route.

The polytechnics, by contrast, were designated in the 1960s as a result of the work of the Robbins Committee (Robbins, 1963). The report laid the basis for a "binary" system of higher education. On the one hand were the universities: autonomous degree-awarding institutions funded by central government via the University Grants Commission taking mostly full-time students in the traditional age group and with a strong commitment to research. On the other hand were the polytechnics and colleges: funded via local education authorities and subject to their control, carrying out substantial proportions of nondegree work alongside degree courses that for the most part have had to be validated externally by a national body, the Council for National Academic Awards (CNAA). The intentions of the Robbins Committee were that public sector institutions should be primarily teaching other than research institutions; that they should provide courses, not necessarily to degree level, of a mainly technical or vocational nature; and that they should have a strong element of part-time provision so as to respond to the needs of students outside the eighteen- to twenty-five-year age group.

In the event, the 1970s in particular saw the rewriting of polytechnic diploma and certificate courses and their submission to the CNAA for validation as full-time degree courses. CNAA validating committees increasingly looked for evidence of research involvement by teaching staff as one of the criteria by which they judged degree submissions.

Taken together, such factors mean that in the mid 1980s the institutions on either side of the binary line are different—but not as different as Robbins envisaged. In 1982-83 the public sector provided "11,000 courses covering 70 different subject areas with a strong emphasis on engineering and business studies." Of the "nearly 400,000 students in these courses, around 45 percent were in part-time courses, nearly 50 percent were in non-degree courses, over 55 percent were mature and over 37 percent women" (NABLAHE, 1984, p. 9). The same report notes that would-be part-time students seeking courses (in public sector) institutions rather than in engineering or business studies to nondegree-level and mature students seeking full-time courses in their locality are often disappointed.

Universities also have seen changes that have altered some of their distinctive features. Research funding to universities has been cut in recent years, and the number of postgraduate students declined by about 15 percent between 1972-73 to 1982-83 (UGC, 1984). The University Grants Commission (UGC) planned for a shift in the science-to-arts ratio from parity in 1979-80 to "a ratio of 52:48 in favor of science" in 1983-84, to be achieved by a reduction in numbers of arts and social science students. In 1982-83 there were in United Kingdom universities 250,000 undergraduates and 45,000 postgraduates (including overseas students). Of these totals, 5,000 undergraduates and 28,000 postgraduates were on part-time courses (UGC, 1984). Thus, "the universities offer the major provision for postgraduate courses—and the majority of part-time first degree students are located in the public sector [e.g., polytechnics] together with the bulk of nondegree provision" (NABLAHE, 1984).

Converging Paths?

Although the overall differences between the two sectors are not as great as the educational planners of the 1960s intended, the differences are there—and are thrown into relief in matters concerning continuing education. But yet another paradox is that within continuing education provision there is a trend for the two types of institution to follow converging paths. Part-time degrees form an example. Despite the small overall proportion of part-time students on first degree courses (17 percent of the total in 1983-84 and three-quarters of those Open University undergraduates), the numbers of part-time degrees on offer have been growing (Tight, 1987). Tight's assessment is that proportions of part-time students increased from 28 to 37 percent between 1970 and 1983. However, of the 615 part-time first-degree courses he identified in the 1985-86 academic year, 72 percent were provided by public sector institutions (nearly one-half in the polytechnics).

The universities could muster only 175 part-time first-degree courses (a figure that included thirty-nine external degrees at the

University of London), and around half of the universities offered no part-time first-degree provision at all.

As the story unfolds into 1989, a good number of those latter universities are considering part-time degree offerings. Polytechnics, meanwhile, are diversifying their part-time degree provision to include the arts, humanities, and social science subjects that for so long have been the staple fare of university extramural departments.

Two themes permeate the whole scene of continuing education in the United Kingdom: (1) the distinction between so-called liberal and so-called vocational education and (2) trends in government funding that evidence changing political evaluations of these two broad types of provision.

In the past, universities have been the main centers for the provision of adult liberal education through their departments of extension studies or extramural studies. Their titles immediately indicate a degree of separation from mainstream university life, and their separate funding mechanisms from the Department of Education and Science has reinforced this. (Universities that have held "responsible body" status—by no means all of them—have had teaching posts for adult education grant-aided by 75 percent from the Department of Education and Science under this mechanism.)

The existence of these departments has concentrated adult liberal provision into the university sector rather than the public sector—and clearly manifests in the type of provision a long-standing university tradition of learning for learning's sake. A side effect of this structure within universities has been that as adult provision has been concentrated in these extramural ("outside the walls") departments, the bulk of other university departments have remained untouched by adult and continuing education philosophies or practices. The exception has been the varying amounts of postexperience provision from departments of engineering, medicine, law, management, education, and the like.

However, the extent of this provision has not been large compared with the extent of adult liberal education provision from universities. In 1985-86 the "top ten" subjects in university adult and continuing education provision (expressed as percentages of courses in all subjects) were: history, 11.04 percent; English literature, 8.63 percent; visual art, 7.42 percent; music, 5.5 percent; biology, 5.1 percent; physical science, 5.09 percent; archaeology and ancient history, 5.05 percent; sociology, 4.68 percent; modern languages and literature, 4.2 percent; and mathematics and computing, 4.11 percent (Jones, 1987). The corresponding percentages for subjects that can be identified as having vocational relevance were: education, 2.85 percent; law, 2.66 percent; other professional studies, 2.38 percent; town and country planning, 1.45 percent; medical studies, 1.17 percent; management studies, 0.97 percent; technology, 0.62

percent; agricultural studies, 0.46 percent; and engineering, 0.36 percent; adding up to 12.92 percent of the total courses provided (Jones, 1987). Four of these vocationally relevant areas (engineering, agricultural studies, technology and management studies) fall within the *bottom* ten of the forty different subject areas offered in 1985-86.

Recent Developments

The last few years have seen rapid and important changes. Department of Education and Science (DES) funding for adult liberal education suffered a progressive cut over the three-year period to 1985-86 and was also subject to a revised funding formula that used numbers recruited to courses as a funding criterion.

At approximately the same time, the DES introduced its PICKUP (professional, industrial, and commercial updating) program, which made new funding available for provision of the postexperience vocational type. The effects of this program were shown initially in the public sector, with a fairly rapid rate of uptake from the colleges (especially colleges of further education) in the first instance. The National Advisory Body for Local Authority Higher Education (NAB-LAHE) made a substantial tranche of funding for PICKUP work available to public sector institutions in mid 1986 as part of a three-year program, which is in its second round of funding in 1987-88. The University Grants Commission followed with a £3 million PICKUP package for universities, for which bids were invited in the spring of 1987, with the first successful initiative commencing at the start of the 1987-88 academic year. The results of bids to the second round of this three-year program (up to another £3 million) were expected at the time of writing (April 1988). Additionally, a much smaller initiative, the Department of Education and Science "PICKUP in Universities" program, was in its last full year of funding in 1987-88. This program provided funds of around £20,000 for one year, decreasing to £7,000 in the second year to enable universities to set up central mechanisms to promote PICKUP provision from throughout their institutions. The level of funding was carefully set *not* to cover the full costs of setting up a new PICKUP post with secretarial backup in order to ensure that successfully bidding universities also dug into their own funds to support PICKUP provision.

Manpower Services Commission Initiatives

All of the PICKUP funding described so far forms part of the Department of Education and Science initiative. However, other types of funding have brought other government departments into the continuing education scene. By far the most significant of these has been the

Department of Employment, which funded the Manpower Services Commission, which in turn has developed a national Adult Training Strategy (discussed elsewhere in this volume). Collaboratively with the Department of Education and Science PICKUP scheme, the Manpower Services Commission has set up schemes to fund 'local collaborative projects.' These are small-scale projects, in which educational institutions and industrial partners collaborate (1) to identify the training needs of the industrial partners and (2) to provide for these needs. The schemes are intended to become self-financing over time.

More ambitiously, the concept of local collaborative projects has been extended to encompass funding for national networks of centers for technology transfer and for consultancy and training on languages and exports. These centers are based on regional consortia of educational institutions from both sides of the "binary" line collaborating with industrial enterprises.

It will be clear that funding has been acting on polytechnics and universities both as a stick and a carrot; the effects of this pushing and pulling are showing in changes at institutional levels. University departments of extramural studies have been changing their names to become, for instance, departments of adult and continuing education. Those universities that lacked "responsible body" status and therefore had no department of extramural studies are setting up an office, a center, or a department of continuing education. PICKUP units and responsibility for local collaborative projects and the technology and language networks are likely to be found within these departments. These renamed, restructured, or simply new units are seeing advantages in breaking down the barriers between adult (liberal) and continuing (vocational) education (Duke, 1988), and in particular some are seeking to involve departments throughout their university in continuing education (Bilham, 1988). A new model is currently in the making in which continuing education is seen as integral to the whole university rather than an activity to be relegated to a separate unit. Paradoxically, polytechnic provision of continuing vocational education through part-time degrees or diplomas has always been provision that has suffused the whole institution. However, short self-financing courses have been the main responsibility of polytechnic units, having titles such as "short courses" or "external courses."

Prospects for Change

While all these measures clearly are having an impact on the continuing education scene, the question must remain as to what the long-term changes will be. The funding initiatives in postexperience education discussed so far are all short term. They have led to a rash of new posts with titles such as "PICKUP liaison officer" or "PICKUP development manager," but many of these posts are offered as one-year contracts only with the hope of extension if the posts generate sufficient income. On the one hand, these posts create a new group of higher education staff. These staff have conditions of service—short-term contracts, contract extension on the basis of job performance, little or no undergraduate teaching, little or no research, no cycles of different activity in term time and vacation time—which are quite distinct from those of their lecturer colleagues and which contain some features that it is clear the government would like to extend to the teaching staff. On the other hand, the likely success of these individuals as agents for change must be called into question precisely because of their insecure tenure. Will PICKUP offices, the scene of thriving activity in 1987, be like ghost towns in a few years time when the PICKUP gold rush is over?

Some universities and polytechnics have used PICKUP money as the seed corn for development programs over the longer term and have underwritten the new PICKUP posts for several years. Other institutions have simply taken the money in the form in which it comes, in which case a PICKUP post either sinks or swims within a one- or two-year period. Recognizing that if it is to be sustained, there is need to incorporate the PICKUP philosophy into institutional life, the Department of Education and Science is now requiring institutions to provide evidence of a strategic approach to PICKUP development across the whole institution, of senior management backing, and of supporting staff development programs. Crucially, evidence of successful outcomes of previous PICKUP funding is important for gaining second- and third-round funding. The Secretary of State for Education and Science announced as a target early in 1987 a fivefold increase in PICKUP provision by 1992 (DES, 1987). Institutions must include in their PICKUP bids business plans, measures of current performance, and forward projections of PICKUP activity. First bids that projected little or no contribution to the government's hoped-for target were unlikely to be successful—as are those second-year bids that show no signs of having achieved a substantial increase in PICKUP provision with the earlier funding received.

Pressures for Change

Perhaps funding alone could not have achieved these changes in the 1980s in a continuing education system that had altered little in the postwar period. The other significant factor has been the prospect of a declining number of eighteen-year-olds in the population. Hence, there is a flurry of activity to attract mature students, and it is here that the old distinctions of "adult" and "continuing" education (or "liberal" and "vocational") are likely to merge over the next five years. The origins for this merger of what have sometimes been treated as polar opposites lie in the potential of new initatives on access, on credit transfer and accumulation (CNAA, 1986), and on the assessment of prior learning (Evans, 1987) to bring about radical changes in the formal procedures of higher educational institutions. Hitherto, the cluster of programs and measures signified by the term *access* have primarily aimed to help adults lacking traditional entry qualifications to gain access to higher education. Usually they offer a preentry program designed to help adults to develop the skills to cope successfully with the demands of a degree course. As with the long-standing facility for university mature student matriculation, the numbers of adults reached are relatively small, and the access gained is to a full-time degree package that is designed around the requirements of the traditional eighteen- to twenty-one-year-old entrant. The new developments in part-time provision could begin to change this, and in particular could begin to respond to arguments from access course tutors that it is higher education institutions that need to change in response to adult learners, rather than the other way round (Entwistle and Wilson, 1987). Credit accumulation and transfer procedures, such as the Council for National Academic Awards' Credit Accumulation and Transfer Scheme (CATS), begin to alter the potential for adults to gain access to degree courses with advanced standing in recognition of prior learning carried out at other institutions. That is to say, choice is opened up well beyond having to attain a complete degree to permit a range of choices from among elements of that degree provision—choices that could be added together serially through credit accumulation. The implications of such measures are the weakening of the barriers between vocational and liberal education, for the purposes of the student would define which type of course was which type of provision. Similarly, divisions between "higher" and "adult and continuing" education would become less relevant as students of the traditional age group and mature students could find themselves pursuing the same course or element of a course.

Other radical measures that are more difficult to implement but on which serious development work is being undertaken include the assessment and accreditation of prior experiential learning and the assessment and accreditation of in-company training schemes. Polytechnics—through the Council of National Academic Awards—are taking the lead here, but universities are following.

New Directions

Contradictions were mentioned at the start of this chapter, and contradictions remain at the end. Measures such as widened access, credit transfer, and the educational guidance services that make it possible for adult students to use such opportunities fully were advocated (along with the idea of independent study) in the 1970s by those at the liberal end of the spectrum of educational politics. These measures are being openly supported in the 1980s as part of a government policy to integrate higher education more closely to the needs of the economy.

A new set of ends is now being pursued by these means. Critics have argued that such measures operate in the real politics of the 1980s as the "managerial conjuring act which allows more students to be taught with fewer resources" (Duke, 1987).

In the final analysis, the world of continuing education in United Kingdom polytechnics and universities is extremely complex. The turn events will take over the next decade does depends not only on government policies, but also institutional policies and actions by key individuals within institutions will play their part. Beyond that, initiatives have been set up that require collaboration between institutions as well as between higher education and industry (the national network of centers for technology transfer and the similar network to promote language/exports training), and these new collaborative structures will provide centers for proactive development of new ventures.

A new actor was waiting in the wings at the time of writing. The former Manpower Services Commission (MSC), renamed the Training Commission, had just announced an initiative to bring "enterprise" into higher education. The funding involved seems likely to be substantial— up to £1 million for each of around 100 higher education institutions over the next five years. The initiative will require successfully bidding institutions to (1) develop opportunities for project-based work (jointly assessed by industry) in the real economy for *all* undergraduates, (2) look for significant measures on mature access and credit transfer, (3) seek active learning methods throughout the institution, and (4) make it a condition of funding that industry make a substantial initial contribution rising to total funding. As with the MSC's Technical and Vocational Education Initiative in secondary schools, the potential is here to make substantial changes in curriculum, teaching methods, and the spirit of each institution. Will universities, colleges, and polytechnics use this as a chance to incorporate continuing education into the heart of institutional practices—with all the implications for becoming student-centered and facilitative of independent learning and for recognizing prior learning? If so, universities and polytechnics in the next decade will be very different institutions from what they are today.

References

Bilham, T. "Organisational Structures and Models." In T. Bilham, M. Carboni, and F. Todd (eds.), *The PICKUP Papers*. Prepared for Second National PICKUP in Universities Conference. London: Department of Education and Science, 1988.

Burgess, T. *Education after School*. Harmondsworth, UK: Penguin, 1977.

Council for National Academic Awards (CNAA). *The Credit Accumulation and Transfer Scheme*. London: CNAA, 1986.

Department of Education and Science (DES). *PICKUP in Progress*, London: DES, Spring 1987.

Duke, C. "Government Funding Policies." In T. Bilham, M. Carboni, and F. Todd (eds.), *The PICKUP Papers*. Prepared for the Second National PICKUP in Universities Conference. London: Department of Education and Science, 1988.

Duke, F. "Degree of Experience: Are the Needs and Expectations of Mature Adults and School-Leavers Compatible?" *Journal of Access Studies*, 1987, *2* (1), 54-63.

Entwistle, J., and Wilson, P. "Access and Quality: Two Responses." *Journal of Access Studies*, 1987, *2* (1), 82-95.

Evans, N. *Assessing Experiential Learning: A Review of Progress and Practice*. York, UK: Longman for FEU Publications, 1987.

Jones, B. (ed.). *Annual Report 1985-86*. Leicester, UK: Universities Council for Adult and Continuing Education, 1987.

National Advisory Body for Local Authority Higher Education (NABLAHE). *A Strategy for Higher Education into the late 1980s and Beyond*. London: NABLAHE, 1984.

Robbins, Lord. *Higher Education: A Report to the Committee Appointed by the Prime Minister under the Chairmanship of Lord Robbins*. London: Her Majesty's Stationery Office, 1963.

Tight, M. "Access and Part-time Under-graduate Study." *Journal of Access Studies*, 1987, *2* (1), 12-24.

University Grants Commission (UGC). *A Strategy for Higher Education into the 1990s*, London: Her Majesty's Stationery Office, 1984.

Young, Lord. "A Nation Learning to Change." *The London Times*, March 26, 1985. Cited in J. McIlroy, "Continuing Education and the Universities in Britain: The Political Context." *International Journal of Lifelong Education*, 1987, *6* (1), 27-59.

Frankie Todd is coordinator for continuing education at the University of York, UK.

Further education in the United Kingdom has been increasingly affected by the activities of the Manpower Services Commission: the commission and the Department of Education and Science have a relationship that is both collaborative and competitive. The system has been subjected to frequent change, and further dramatic change is imminent.

Continuing Education in Colleges of Further Education

Laurie S. Piper

Historical Background

The most rapid expansion of the further education system took place after the 1944 Education Act, the purpose of which was to educate and train those who would rebuild the British Economy after World War II. Thus, the system of poststatutory (over sixteen years of age) education in the United Kingdom, as a whole, now consists for 46 universities, 30 polytechnics, 658 other colleges, 57 "government-assisted institutions," and 4,513 adult education centers (DES, 1986). Within the "other colleges" category, about 500 can be identified broadly as the further education colleges.

When the Department of Education and Science (DES) and the Manpower Services Commission (MSC) jointly initiated the Review of Vocational Qualifications in 1986 (DES/MSC, 1986), it was discovered that about 600 of these organizations were offering 6,000 different qualifications in the United Kingdom, some with overlap and duplication, to give a total of about 1.75 million awards annually. Some 250 professional bodies set examinations, and for those 76 that have Royal Charters, this is important, since these examinations give their members legal license to practice their professions (for example, doctors, lawyers, engineers). It is, therefore, not surprising that the Review of Vocational Qualifications Report recommended the rapid establishment of a National Council for Vocational Qualifications in an attempt to rationalize a most confusing situation. The National Council for Vocational Qualifications came into being in October 1986 and is struggling to produce a rational system in which all qualifications are located within one of several levels, with "bridges and pathways" linking them in such a way that examination candidates of the future will be able to gain credit at each stage and progress their education and training throughout their careers without duplication or repetition. The main thrust lies in devising ways of assessing the competence of individuals to perform their jobs effectively (NCVQ, 1987).

With such a complex system of examining bodies, apparently offering a virtually unlimited array of qualifications, most people must hold qualifications, and Britain must surely be the world's industrial leader, or at least be well up among the leaders, but nothing could be further from the truth. Although she led the world at the time of the Industrial Revolution, there were signs that Britain was losing her industrial supremacy well back in the nineteenth century, and, if anything, the overall picture has further deteriorated in recent times. Why should this be so?

Inertia in the System

For many years, the government has been convinced that much of British industry was not really interested in training: training needs were not being accurately identified or met. Many firms did not send their employees on courses, and if they did, they tended to accept what colleges chose to offer rather than to determine and demand what was really necessary. When skilled workers were suddenly required, industry tended to "poach" them from competitors rather than produce them through well-planned training programs. Indeed, the majority of firms, if they trained their employees at all, did so only on an ad hoc basis. The colleges, on their part, still offered traditional full-time and part-time courses leading to the formal qualifications of the national and regional examining bodies. Courses were infrequently updated, and the offerings were strictly confined within a clearly defined academic year: short updating courses were comparatively rare. In brief, colleges were neither flexible nor responsive. As a consequence, only recently it has been estimated that no more than 40 percent of the United Kingdom work force hold qualifications relevant to their employment (OPCS, 1986).

In an attempt to analyze the true needs of industry and to construct training programs to meet them, the government passed the Industrial Training Act of 1964, which provided for the creation of a range of industrial training boards covering most of the major industries in Britain. The boards were financed largely by statutory levies that they imposed on their industries, and firms were given grants by the boards for operating approved training schemes. Nevertheless, the levy/grant system was cumbersome and, although some boards were very much more successful than others, the system as a whole did not fully achieve its intended potential. Many firms were still not convinced of the need to train and saw the boards as an unnecessary bureaucracy. The act, however, did improve flexibility in college attitudes and increase their willingness to offer more short courses tailor-made to meet specific needs. At the peak, there were about thirty statutory and voluntary industrial training boards, but in recent years most have been disbanded, leaving only eight.

The Manpower Services Commission

The most significant step for change was taken in 1972 when the Department of Employment issued its discussion document "Training for the Future," which embraced proposals for a massive expansion in training by United Kingdom standards, not only for school leavers but also for adults. The supremacy of the Department of Education and Science (DES) as an effective organizer of education and training for industry and commerce in the modern world was being challenged by another government department. The legislation was introduced in 1973 (DES, 1973), in the Employment and Training Act, and the Manpower Services Commission (MSC) came into being on January 1, 1974. Until 1990 the main objectives of the commission are to be concerned with improving the efficiency and effectiveness of industry through the development of a skilled and adaptable work force, including management.

Among its early training initiatives, which immediately affected the work of further education colleges, the Manpower Services Commission introduced the Youth Opportunities Program to provide up to a year of training and work-based experience for unemployed school leavers, and a much smaller Unified Vocational Preparation Scheme to give a foundation of training and related further education to young people in jobs where little or no training would otherwise have been available. Both programs were subsumed under the Youth Training Scheme in 1983. To enable adults to obtain a first qualification, or to update their skills, the Training Opportunities Scheme was introduced, in which trainees usually attended college courses to obtain qualifications. This scheme was also transitory, eventually to be absorbed within the Job Training Program.

The above changes were first heralded in May 1981, when the

Manpower Services Commission issued a major consultative document entitled *A New Training Initiative*, which has largely become the guiding light for current policy. Highlighting again the inadequacy of the British system, the document set out the following three primary objectives:

1. To develop occupational training, including apprenticeship, in such a way as to enable people entering at different ages and with different educational attainments to acquire agreed standards of skill appropriate to the jobs available and to provide them with a basis for progression through further learning.

2. To move toward a position where all young people under the age of eighteen have the opportunity either of continuing in full-time education or of entering training or a period of planned work experience combining work-related training and education.

3. To open up widespread opportunities for adults, whether employed, unemployed, or returning to work, to acquire, increase, or update their skills and knowledge during the course of their working lives.

The Secretaries of State for Employment and for Education and Science presented the results of their consultations to Parliament in the White Paper entitled *A New Training Initiative: An Agenda for Action* (MSC, 1981). In essence, the White Paper paved the way for the following initiatives, which have formed the basis for much of the Manpower Services Commission work since then:

1. The development of a Youth Training Scheme to replace the Youth Opportunities Program and the Unified Vocational Preparation Scheme, which would provide one year of training for all those leaving school at sixteen who were without jobs.
2. Incentives to employers to provide better training.
3. The establishment of an "Open Tech" program to produce distance learning materials.
4. The development of recognized standards in all main craft, technician, and many professional skills, to replace traditional apprenticeships.
5. Improvements in the preparation for working life in initial full-time education.
6. More opportunities for vocationally relevant courses for those remaining in full-time education.
7. Better coordination of training and vocational education provision nationally and locally.

The primary objectives set out in the *New Training Initiative* and the *Agenda for Action* that arose from them clearly demonstrated the government's intention to create a new, flexible system of initial and continuing education and training for the people throughout their lives. Time-serving apprenticeships and formal examinations were to be replaced, where appropriate, by tests for skills competency; training in the workplace was to become as important—if not more so—than training off the job. There was to be training for all, and employers were expected to become partners in the education and training system and to commit time and money to the process.

Within this strategy, in an educational sense, the divide between initial and continuing education/training became blurred. Having made the point, however, space will not permit a review of the provision for the sixteen- to eighteen-year age group, which includes the "flagship" of Manpower Services Commission activity, the Youth Training Scheme. Instead, the remainder of this chapter will be concerned with the Manpower Services Commission and the Department of Education and Science initiatives primarily intended for adults—that is, those over eighteen years of age—since these can be more clearly identified within a more conventional definition of continuing education.

Manpower Services Commission Adult Training Schemes

In 1985 the Manpower Services Commission restructured its adult training strategies for those eighteen years of age and over. The long-established Training Opportunities Scheme was replaced by two new initiatives designed to be more flexible in meeting local needs.

The smaller of the two schemes, the Wider Opportunities Training Program, offers courses to help the unemployed get back to work. These courses are flexible in terms of duration, mode of attendance, and content, as long as they enhance the employment prospects of those who attend. Among the more interesting offerings are courses for women who wish to return to work.

The larger initiative, the Job Training Program, encompasses a range of initiatives, the most important of which are concerned with the development of management, supervisory, and business skills generally, especially for those who have started or wish to start their own business ventures. Courses on specific industrial/commercial skills are also available, either full time or part time, lasting up to a maximum period of one year according to need.

A more recent venture, the New Job Training Scheme, which superceded a similarly named earlier initiative, was intended to provide tailor-made training packages as much as possible "on demand" for the unemployed between the ages of eighteen and twenty-five years. A six-month training entitlement at the workplace, with the opportunity to obtain an appropriate, job-related qualification, forms the basis of this scheme. Many difficulties arose because of the requirement to provide a qualification, since most course providers cannot run courses for a small number of students on demand and still maintain a cost-effective operation; as yet there are insufficient distance learning packages available to meet the potential demand. The MSC's "Open Tech" project did not live up to expectations in producing distance learning material for the mass market, and the Open College has made a very slow start (see Chapter Eight, this volume).

Manpower Services Commission sponsorship for Adult Training Schemes has risen sharply in recent years. In 1983-84 just over 80,000 trainees entered Training Opportunities Scheme courses, whereas in 1986-87 the total numbers entering the schemes mentioned above exceeded 390,000 (MSC, 1987). Looking at the population as a whole, these numbers are not great, but it is significant to note that over 65 percent of the training was carried out without the aid of the further education service, whereas little more than a decade ago, virtually all would have been done by further education colleges.

In addition to the above schemes, which form part of the Manpower Services Commission's Adult Training Strategy, the commission has introduced two other partially funded programs designed largely to meet the continuing education needs of existing employees: the local employers' networks and local collaborative projects. Local employers' networks are industry-led consortia of employers, partially funded to research their joint training needs and to identify training programs with appropriate providers. After an initial injection of MSC funds, they are expected to become self-supporting. Generally, the scheme finds limited support from employers. Local collaborative projects are similar, but in their case the consortium works together more as a partnership with the education service in planning and delivery of the programs. By mid 1987 there were 400 college-employer training partnerships, involving 300 colleges, polytechnics, and universities, and more than 2,500 firms (MSC, 1987).

Enterprise Schemes and the Community Program

The schemes discussed above were developed under the aegis of the Vocational Education and Training Group of the MSC, but some, which also involve training, were developed by the Employment and Enterprise Group.

The Enterprise Allowance Scheme, launched in 1983, makes limited funds available to unemployed persons who have the necessary skills and willingness to set up small businesses, provided that they can first find £1,000 to invest in their own business. By March 1986 nearly 134,000 people had benefited and, in 1986-87, the MSC spent £150 million on the scheme. The Community Program, set up and funded by

MSC to carry out work for the benefit of the community, which would otherwise not be done due to a lack of resources, is another feature of the work of the Employment and Enterprise Group. This provides full-time or part-time (75 percent are part-time) employment for the long-term unemployed, which lasts for twelve months. Annually, about 300,000 people are encompassed by the scheme; about one-third of those leaving the scheme enter full-time employment. Business skills training is an important feature of the Enterprise Allowance Scheme, whereas a limited variety of training opportunities appropriate to the work at hand is a minor feature of Community Program schemes. Colleges and private providers share this training between them. Toward the end of 1987, however, greater emphasis was placed on training within the Community Program.

Skillcenters

MSC-funded skillcenters—free-standing adult training centers—are increasingly competing with further education colleges and have become very commercially oriented since 1983, when they were incorporated within the Skills Training Agency, another division of the MSC. There are about sixty Skillcenters in England, Wales, and Scotland, which are now diversifying from the teaching of craft skills into the area of new technology. In this context, the Skills Training Agency has created seventeen new technology Access Centers since 1985. Many Skillcenters also offer mobile training services to industry: they are providers of off-the-job training, and most now act as examination centers. During 1986-87, about 33,000 people received training in Skillcenters, and another 16,000 via the mobile training service. Nevertheless, within a few years, most Skillcenters will be in a crisis situation as central funding is further reduced and employers are expected to bear more of the cost.

**Professional, Industrial, and Commercial Updating—
DES Initiative**

Spurred on by the MSC's pressures for lifelong updating and retraining through the Adult Training Strategy, DES launched its own initiative in 1982. Professional, industrial, and commercial updating, "PICKUP," as the scheme was designated, is aimed at all institutions offering poststatutory education—not just the further education colleges but polytechnics, other major colleges, and the universities. The scheme promotes the preparation and delivery of short, full-cost recovery courses, tailored to meet the updating needs of specific groups of employees, whether technical, supervisory, or management. The government provides funds to assist in the development of PICKUP courses, particularly for training further education college staff in the techniques required for highly effective short-course preparation and delivery. About £3 million in grants was injected into the PICKUP initiative by government in 1987-88, and most regions within the United Kingdom now have development officers whose job it is to stimulate and steer the scheme in line with government policy. A national computer catalogue is available to employers, giving information about courses available, their location, and cost.

To date, many local further education colleges have responded less vigorously to the PICKUP challenge than have the polytechnics and universities, and yet these colleges are ideally suited to assist firms situated within their catchment areas, since they generally have staff with the appropriate expertise to provide the courses required.

In addition, in 1989 selected groups of colleges, polytechnics, and universities that have already proved their ability to operate continuing education courses in the field of "new technology" are to be brought together in partnership with industry, under the banner of local collaborative project schemes, to form a network of about nine regional new technology centers, funded jointly by PICKUP, the Manpower Services Commission, and the Department of Trade and Industry. Each will receive an initial grant of £100,000 but will be expected to become self-funding within several years.

Continuing education via PICKUP is growing by about 11 percent per year overall, but in those institutions that have made a positive commitment to adult training, the average growth is about 40 percent annually. DES intends to press for a fivefold increase over the next five years, and this year has budgeted to inject £12.25 million into the scheme (DES, 1987). Twenty-eight universities have already been allocated a total of £9 million, and twenty-two polytechnics and twenty large, and eight medium-sized further education colleges will share £3 million. Since this represents only a small part of the further education system, clearly the majority of colleges have a long way to go.

Traditional Continuing Education in Further Education and Adult Education Centers

As it has always done, the further education system still provides extension and updating courses for employed adults on a full-time, day-release, or evening basis across the entire range of vocational and academic disciplines, and the students attending vastly outnumber the trainees on MSC schemes. From the statistics, it is virtually impossible to separate those who are adding to postschool education to obtain additional, higher-level qualifications from those who are studying for

Table 1. Totals by Age Groups Attending Further Education (in thousands)

Category	19-20	21-24	Over 25
Full-time NAFE[a]	30	17	30
Full-time AFE[a]	108	70	44
Part-time NAFE	90	46	217
Part-time AFE	37	43	62
Evening NAFE[b]	144	399	1,539
Evening AFE	3	12	33

[a] Advanced further education (AFE) is higher education not normally available to those under the age of eighteen years. It covers higher diploma/certificate and graduate-level studies. Nonadvanced further education (NAFE) covers basic craft/technician training. It is available to anyone with appropriate entry qualifications after the age of sixteen (the earliest age at which people can leave school).
[b] Includes those in Adult Education Centers.

first qualifications, although it is reasonable to assume that the higher proportion of those beyond the age of eighteen must fall into the former category. The figures from 1983-84 are seen in Table 1.

Although many further education colleges contain departments of adult education, a larger number of free-standing adult education centers lie outside the control of colleges. Within colleges, most vocational continuing education takes place in the specialist departments, whereas the recreational/leisure courses are usually the preserve of a separate adult education department. Free-standing adult education centers seldom have access to the facilities required to provide more than a sprinkling of vocational courses, and these are usually at a basic level. Thus, they, too, usually concentrate on nonvocational activity, leaving the vocational work to the colleges. There are, however, a number of areas where adult education centers offer some elementary vocational courses, particularly in the areas of secretarial studies and, more recently, in introductory courses for small businesses and computing.

Increasingly, institutions are working together in partnership, displaying a growing willingness to accept previous examination successes and experience when accumulating credits toward qualifications for individuals so that mature students, in particular, do not have to retread the same ground in their studies toward formal qualifications. The universities and polytechnics are not particularly active in these "credit transfer" arrangements (see Chapter Three, this volume). These sectors are working increasingly with further education colleges to provide "access" courses in addition to their traditional wide range of adult education courses to give adults entry to higher education via nontraditional routes. All of these initiatives are strongly encouraged by the University Grants Commission, the National Advisory Body for

Public Sector Higher Education, and the Council for National Academic Awards. A more flexible approach is, at least, emerging, and some exciting institutional networks are being established.

Nevertheless, it has to be admitted that the growing willingness to admit nontraditionally qualified adults to higher education arises partially because the number leaving school by 1991 will have reduced by nearly 20 percent over a five-year period.

Continuing Education of Further Education Teachers and Trainers

The continuing education of teachers (usually called "staff development") has, at the advanced level, for many years been the preserve of certain higher education institutions (the "providers") designated by DES and supplemented at a regional and local level by a range of short courses that, in total, were quite inadequate to meet the needs of accelerating change. Those who wished to gain higher-level qualifications usually had to attend an expensive period of study leave at one of the provider institutions. Although funding was available in many cases through the DES-controlled, now defunct advanced courses "pool," the system lacked flexibility and responsiveness. New arrangements have, therefore, been introduced over the last few years whereby DES provides the local education authorities with funds that have to be spent on teacher development. Some priority areas are defined nationally and some locally. For the first time, local authorities and their colleges are required to produce and implement staff development plans for which specific funding is available.

MSC, however, realized that staff that were delivering its schemes would be in need of frequent updating, and not being hidebound with prejudice and tradition, set up, in 1982–83, a nationwide network of forty-four Accredited Training Centers, about half of which are run by colleges. The centers offer some qualifying courses for trainers, with the main thrust of center activity being geared to short, specialist courses lasting up to a few days, which are at present fully funded by MSC. Recently, these centers have been deeply involved in preparing organizations operating as Youth Training Scheme managing agents for "approved training organization" status, without which they cannot operate as managing agents (that is, training providers) for the Youth Training Scheme. These centers also mount courses or a consultancy service to meet identified staff training needs at times and places suitable for their clients. In short, they are responsive and flexible and thus will probably be used increasingly by organizations other than MSC managing agents. In 1986–87, more than 170,000 trainers attended

Accredited Center courses and, of these, more than 100,000 were first-line supervisors involved in the delivery of the Youth Training Scheme.

What About the Future?

In the present political and economic climate, making predictions about the long-term future of any part of the educational/training system is a very risky business. By the time this volume appears in print, some of the current schemes discussed will already have been discontinued in favor of other initiatives; such is the rate of change. A major new education act should be on the statute books and will transfer the greater part of nonuniversity higher education from local to central government control.

While most further education colleges are likely to remain under local education authority control, they will be given greater autonomy and greatly increased industrial representation on governing bodies. Large numbers of institutions, particularly in higher education, will become corporate bodies in the government's perpetual thrust toward privatization. Institutions will need to become increasingly responsive and efficient if they are to compete with the private sector training organizations; the number of short, full-cost, continuing education courses is likely to increase significantly in both public and private sector institutions, and, marketing will become increasingly important.

In October 1987, dramatic changes were announced about the future role of the MSC, and these have been confirmed in a recent White Paper *Training for Employment* (MSC, 1988). In short, under the new title of Training Commission, subsequently the Training Agency, it will maintain responsibility for all programs involving training. In September 1988, a new initiative for adults, designated "employment training," will start by bringing together all the Training Commission's initiatives for training adults into what will essentially be one scheme. This will mean that many training providers and Community Program agents will have to come together to form fewer but larger organizations, designated "training managers," either by combination or federation, to deliver the adult training program of the future, which will carry a six- to twelve-month training entitlement. "Employment training" poses many challenges, and the problems requiring solution will be legion. In time, there can be little doubt that this new initiative and the Youth Training Scheme will merge to form an education continuum from age sixteen onward. If this new scheme fails, the Training Commission might itself cease to exist.

Perhaps, in the longer term, the government may also heed the cries of the many educators and trainers who believe that vocational (and perhaps nonvocational) education and training after age sixteen must eventually become the responsibility of a single government department, if all the many initiatives are to be sensibly rationalized, organized, and delivered in the most effective manner. Hopefully, this would do much to introduce some stability into the education/training systems in the United Kingdom, which are, at present, subject to unreasonably frequent levels of change.

References

Department of Education and Science (DES). *The Employment and Training Act 1973*. London: Her Majesty's Stationery Office, 1973.
Department of Education and Science (DES). *Education Statistics for the United Kingdom*. London: Her Majesty's Stationery Office, 1986.
Department of Education and Science (DES). *PICKUP in Progress*. London: DES, 1987.
Department of Education and Science/Manpower Services Commission (DES/MSC). *Review of Vocational Qualifications in England and Wales, DES/MSC Joint Report*. London: Her Majesty's Stationery Office, 1986.
Manpower Services Commission (MSC). *A New Training Initiative: An Agenda for Action*. London: MSC, 1981.
Manpower Service Commission (MSC). *Training for Employment*. London: MSC, 1987.
National Council for Vocational Qualifications (NCVQ) in England, Wales, and Northern Ireland. *Purpose and Aims*. London: Her Majesty's Stationery Office, 1987.
Office of Population Censuses and Surveys (OPCS). *Labour Force Survey 1983/1984*. London: OPCS, 1986.

Laurie S. Piper is principal of Cornwall College of Further and Higher Education, UK.

Since 1975 trade union representatives have enjoyed rights to paid educational leave to attend trade union courses funded—but not controlled—by the government.

Continuing Education in the Trade Union Movement

John Holford

Developments in British trade union education since the 1960s have been the products of industrial and economic, as well as educational, policy. Business and government, as well as trade unions and educational organizations, have played a part in making policies and in determining the effectiveness of provision. This chapter surveys the main developments in trade union education since the 1960s, the shape of current provision, and some recent issues and debates. It focuses on provision made under the Trades Union Congress (TUC) education scheme, which dominates the field. (The TUC is a trade union organization analogous to the AFL-CIO.)

The Development of a TUC Policy

During the 1960s and early 1970s, the British trade union movement evolved a new formula for educating trade unionists. The TUC, along with a few of the larger unions affiliated to it, began to develop their own provision shortly after World War II. Their courses were targeted, in the main, at full-time union officials and senior lay workplace representatives, concentrating on practical industrial relations and bargaining issues.

P. Jarvis (ed.). *Britain: Policy and Practice in Continuing Education.*
New Directions for Continuing Education, no. 40. San Francisco: Jossey-Bass, Winter 1988.

Policy Formation. The period of policy formulation that followed occurred amid the years of postwar "full employment" and prosperity, when workplace trade union organization became widespread, especially in the private sector of the manufacturing industry. It also coincided with the zenith of British trade unions' political influence and the development (by Conservative as well as Labor governments) of mechanisms designed to weld trade unionism into the policy-making structures of the body politic. During these years, the TUC's general approach reflected a relatively broad national consensus on economic and industrial policy: it accepted that national economic problems, particularly inflation, were in part due to "wage drift" in a tight labor market where strong workplace organization could win wage increases greater than national norms. Associated with this was concern that some shop stewards—lay workplace trade union representatives—might use such organization in the pursuit of aims that differed from those nationally established by their unions. And the TUC's 1960s debate on trade union education also coincided with a major national debate on the reform of industrial relations, which culminated in the Royal Commission on Trade Unions and Employers Associations' report (1968). The core of this report was the view that Britain had "two systems of industrial relations"—formal and informal—that were often at odds with one another. The informal (which needed to be controlled) was represented in particular by the actual behavior of shop stewards and managers at the workplace level

The TUC Strategy. The strategy evolved by the TUC during the 1960s reflected this atmosphere but was also educationally innovative. Stated most clearly in the Working Party Report *Training Shop Stewards* (TUC 1968), it had several key features. First, a strong case was made for education (or training) against those who held that union representatives could learn from experience alone. Second, shop stewards (and other union lay workplace representatives) were identified as the key stratum to which training should be directed. Until then, provision had been more broadly aimed—merely at trade union members—although in practice, students were generally active or committed in trade unions or labor politics. Third, there was a series of proposals on teaching and learning. Course content should be related to the main activities undertaken by shop stewards: understanding rules, policies, agreements, and so forth; specialized knowledge of industrial law, management techniques, and the like; and skills related to communication, collecting and analyzing information, and effective presentation of cases. On teaching methods, lectures were opposed as generally unsuitable: more active, if more time-consuming, methods such as group discussion, role plays, and case studies—which "till, rather than simply cover, the ground" (TUC 1968, p. 27)—were preferred.

Fourth, several important organizational developments were

recommended. A shift in method of delivery from evening and weekend to day-release courses would encourage the less-committed shop steward to attend. The TUC should provide various teaching materials. Tutors needed training in teaching methods—particularly union officials who might be asked to contribute to the teaching of courses. Publicly funded educational bodies—not only the Workers' Educational Association (WEA) but the further education colleges and university extramural departments—were encouraged to involve themselves in trade union education.

Problem of Implementation

By the end of the 1960s, the TUC had a firm policy on education for trade unionists and a general strategy for its development, covering educational as well as institutional aspects. But in certain areas, policy was underdeveloped. Above all, there was ambivalence on the question of control. Certainly, the TUC was attempting to set benchmarks of acceptable practice, and to implement mechanisms to make these effective. But it also accepted that public educational bodies should be involved (a definite shift from the "independent working-class education" approach). And, in pursuit of employers' agreement to day release, the TUC in 1963 and 1967 reached agreement with the major employers' associations on statements accepting that employers should have a say in deciding whether a course was suitable for shop stewards who were their employees. The "essential criterion" was that employers and unions should see the course "as contributing to the promotion of sound industrial relations" (TUC, 1968, p. 86).

Joint Training. This ambivalence was tested in the early 1970s when the Commission on Industrial Relations (CIR), established by the Conservative government, reported on industrial relations training (CIR, 1972). (As part of its general opposition to that government's policy on industrial relations and trade unions, the TUC withdrew cooperation from the commission.) Much of the CIR report was unexceptionable, but there were two main areas of contention. The report accepted that unions were responsible for training their shop stewards but also argued: "Much of the responsibility for shop steward training can only be effectively carried out in conjunction with employers" (CIR, 1972, p. 57). And it recommended that shop stewards should be trained separately in industrial relations and in their role as union representatives. These recommendations were rejected by the TUC (1973), which now asserted strongly that responsibility for the training of shop stewards rested as of right with trade unions and that training in industrial relations and trade union roles were inseparable.

The Labor Government. With the response to the CIR report, the trade union movement had developed a coherent educational policy. Two problems remained, however, if the need for employers' support was to be avoided: the financing of provision and the release of shop stewards for courses. The return of the Labor government in 1974 provided solutions. First, the 1975 Employment Protection Act gave union representatives a statutory right to a "reasonable" amount of paid educational leave for training "relevant" to their industrial relations functions and approved by the TUC or their trade union. This right was supported by a Code of Practice giving official guidance on the implementation of the act. Second, the government made a grant to the TUC to enable it to pay the fees of students in certain courses (approved by the TUC) promoted by public educational bodies, and toward course development and tutor training work carried out by the TUC itself. The first grant (£400,000) was made in 1976; though modest in itself, and in comparison with expenditures on management education and training, it was the basis for a revolution in trade union education.

Growth of the Scheme. In the year 1973-74, 8,731 students attended 643 day release courses promoted through the TUC; by 1976-77, 21,372 students attended 1,560 such courses; in 1978-79 (the peak year to date), there were 43,856 students in 3,100 courses. Yet even this expansion could be little more than a start in relation to the number of potential students. About 300,000 was a common estimate for the number of shop stewards in the later 1970s. To this, however, should be added allowances for safety representatives, a union position that existed in substantial numbers only after health and safety legislation in the mid 1970s (TUC figures above include health and safety courses), and for turnover, averaging perhaps 20 or 30 percent each year.

Central to the developing TUC strategy was cooperation with public educational bodies. A number of WEA, university extramural, and technical college tutors had been working with trade unions and the TUC for some time, but the expansion now envisaged required the deployment of far greater teaching resources. But this brought a number of difficulties. The bulk of tutors in technical (now commonly termed "further education") colleges with expertise in industrial relations had gained this by teaching courses for managers; there was concern about their commitment to trade unionism. Would they practice the active learning methods the TUC favored? It was unclear, too, whether their timetables would allow them to devote whole days to union teaching.

Course Development. These problems were tackled in four main measures. First, a course development unit was established at the TUC Training College. Second, its staff were charged with the task of producing course materials. In 1977 a detailed, printed package had been developed for the *Introductory Course for Union Representatives,* running to well over 200 pages. Over the following two or three years came similarly substantial packages on *Rights at Work, Health and Safety at Work, Bargaining Information,* and *Work Study, Productivity, and Pay,* as well as special editions of the *Introductory* pack designed for representatives in local government and the National Health Service. These packages included not only information but specimen learning activities. The typical activity became discussion in small groups (three or four strong) of an issue; often one member of the group took notes of the discussion and then reported on the main points raised in his or her group (thus also practicing practical skills of importance to shop stewards). Also produced were specimen case studies and role plays. And with each package came extensive guidance notes for tutors (and indeed, until the early 1980s, a detailed specimen timetable to which tutors were broadly assumed to adhere).

Tutor Training. Third, the course development unit spearheaded a substantial program of tutor training. Each year, several five-day, residential briefings for tutors were held: it became policy that courses would be approved only if taught by tutors who had attended a briefing related to the course in question. These measures had an important effect on quality control; certain tutors felt that they were also used to set the parameters of politically or ideologically acceptable content. (This is the dominant refrain of recent articles by John McIlroy (1985a, b). Finally, colleges and WEA districts were encouraged to appoint full-time staff devoted to trade union education; the TUC concentrated its provision in certain colleges and WEA districts, designating some of the former "Trade Union Studies Centers."

TUC Education in the Eighties

This carefully contrived structure was hardly in place before it had to withstand the typhoon that followed the election of the Conservative government in 1979. The government's economic policies led to widespread closures and to burgeoning unemployment; its industrial relations legislation seriously curtailed trade union rights and weakened the moral standing of unions. Recruitment to union courses fell. Although the legal right to paid release remained, increasing practical difficulties were placed in the way of shop stewards and safety representatives seeking to avail themselves of these rights; many took the easy option and did not apply. In 1979-80, 3,032 TUC day-release courses enrolled 38,981 students; six years later (in 1985-86), there were only 1,541 courses and 18,752 day release students.

The background to British trade union education in the 1980s has thus been declining student demand for day-release courses. Inevitably, this has seriously eroded the teaching resources built up in colleges, polytechnics, WEA districts, and extramural departments. But it has also been a period of declining union membership, of union retreat: union education's attempts to reassess its role, and to establish an effective strategy for this new world, have taken place within a wider debate about unions' role and methods.

The 1987 Review. There have been several important developments in the 1980s, but the overwhelming feature is continuity. Trade union education must be committed to trade union aims and objectives; it should assist representatives in carrying out their functions; it should promote union organization. While it "will contribute to . . . individual development, it must reinforce the collective nature of lay representatives' functions and responsibilities"; it "should bring together representatives from different unions, occupations, industries and establishments" (TUC, 1987, p. 8). There is no educationally sensible separation to be made between representatives' industrial relations and trade union functions. Trade unions alone should be responsible for determining the objectives and methods of training. Training should "be conducted sympathetically and seek to establish confidence and motivation"; it should take place in an educational setting free from undue employer influence. It is "adult education in its fullest sense," justifying the allocation of public funds. All these policies were considered "equally valid today."

In practical terms, the program of day-release courses (of ten days' duration) has continued to be the core of union educational provision: multiunion courses for shop stewards and safety representatives. There has been a continuing commitment to developing course materials, and the "packs" for shop stewards and health and safety courses have each undergone one major and several minor revisions. But a number of significant innovations reflect in various ways the concerns and experiences of the 1980s. We can present only a few examples here.

Equal Opportunities. First, far greater emphasis has been placed on equal opportunities. Although in principle always a matter for consideration in courses, the 1980s have seen important developments. The TUC in 1980 introduced "bridging" courses for women (of three to five days' duration and timed to fit in with the school day). These were designed to encourage more women to become involved in the ten-day courses and to develop the skills and confidence to take on union offices. They are taught by women; an emphasis is placed on providing a relaxed, noncompetitive atmosphere. From about 1983, further short courses have been promoted specifically for women: "Women and Pensions," "Women and Sexual Harassment at Work," "Women and Health at Work," and "Equal Pay for Work of Equal Value." Partly as a result (though partly due to shifts in occupational and industrial structure), the proportion of women attending TUC day-release courses has risen from 7 percent (1978) to 24 percent (1987). However, major weaknesses remain.

For instance, there are relatively few women tutors and childcare is too frequently unavailable to students attending trade union courses.

Race has also become a priority. In 1983 the *The TUC Workbook on Racism* was published. This was to be used both in general trade union courses and in a specific program of courses on "Tackling Racism." Some courses are advertised (and some materials available) in various ethnic minority languages. However, the effectiveness of this program is difficult to gauge, partly because no ethnic monitoring of students was carried out (until 1986). Greater emphasis has also been placed on disability.

New Target Groups. Second, as areas of traditional union strength have been eroded, so courses have tried to respond to the needs of occupations where unionism is of more recent origin, and often apparently weaker. Recent research suggests that despite the large-scale erosion of union membership, and the reduction in the number of union representatives in manufacturing and some private services, the overall number of union representatives *increased* slightly in the early 1980s, especially in the public sector. Thus, to some degree the assumptions of early editions of the TUC materials—that most shop stewards are manual workers and have well-established procedures agreeing with management—have shifted. Courses are now far more concerned with the basics of how to establish organization, sustain members' commitment, and make the union presence felt with uncooperative management.

Short Courses. Third, following an important policy shift (the government in 1984-85 made funds available to the TUC for short courses), there has been a burgeoning of courses related to the needs of specific unions, sectors, and issues. TUC education has been able to cooperate far more closely with the developing educational provision of individual unions. Such programs have been accompanied by special course materials, often produced in association with educational staff of the unions concerned. Short courses have also enabled trade union studies tutors in WEA districts and colleges to take a more active role in course development, approaching union organizations in their areas, identifying their training requirements, and designing appropriate courses.

Membership Education. Fourth, in the early 1980s there was a strong reaction among trade union educators against providing education just for union representatives. Many union problems seemed to stem from members not understanding unions' role and aims; it appeared sensible to provide education for union members as well. Of course, the resources available for any significant venture in "membership education"—with about 10 million trade union members—would be vast, and state funding has been available only for the training of representatives. So union representatives were encouraged to attend short courses on educational methods and to begin organizing and leading discussion groups in their workplaces—at best, a very qualified success. More recently, this approach has been strengthened by the piloting (from 1987) of a TUC "Open School" aiming to offer distance learning both individually on the postal course model and through study groups.

Methods. The early 1980s saw a subtle but significant swing in the area of methods. Of course, the TUC had long favored active, participative, "student-centered" learning methods. But in these years, a current of opinion developed in the TUC's course development unit—supported by a significant sector of tutors around the country—that sought to reduce the role of the tutor as expert. To overstate the case, there was a shift from the clearly correct view that union representatives' deep experience of workplace industrial relations is a vital learning resource to the controversial assertion that students' prior knowledge is all the information that a course required. The tutor sometimes seemed a very optional extra. This was associated with a tendency to play down the importance of subject matter or content: implicitly, the essence was that students should cooperatively solve problems.

Strangely, perhaps, it was around this issue that some of the most heated debate within British trade union education has developed. In practice, some argued, tutors were largely abandoning responsibility for courses to course members; some tutors also questioned how far such methods could fulfill their own aims or lead to effective learning. But the debate also spilled into the area of curriculum control and into the vexing question of the political content of the curriculum. Paradoxically, it was argued that the increased use of course committees—apparently, greater student control—increased central control over the curriculum, for the only immutable element of the course would be the printed pack. And the chief factors that structured the central curriculum, it was suggested, would be the term of the TUC's funding relationship with the state and the TUC's own internal politics—its constant need to balance the objectives of its various member unions.

Political Education. Trade union studies tutors tend to see the trade union movement in a political perspective, and there has long been a tension between a desire for political education and the focus on the workplace as the basis of union education. The latter position is, of course, justified partly by the educational imperative of dealing (or at least starting) with issues relating to students' immediate experience. But there is a deeper source of tension. The origins of public funding for trade union education are to be found—as we have seen—not so much in the state's educational policy as in its industrial relations and economic policy. Within educational circles, even in government, an ethos remains: that adult education cannot exclude, and may require, the examination of controversial issues; students may, after examining a range of issues, yet prefer a course of action that is unattractive to government. But industrial relations policy is less concerned with the process of educating union representatives than with its outcome: "using training of stewards as part of a planned move to more orderly industrial relations" as the Royal Commission (1968, p. 191) has put it. In short, if oversimply, education operates with a notion of legitimate activity based on impartiality between, and fair consideration of, contending arguments. Notions of what is legitimate in industrial relations have shifted markedly over recent years, but even at best (that is, when unions were most positively regarded), they started from the objective of ensuring national economic prosperity within an economy based on private ownership and profit.

A Secure Future?

British trade union education grew in little more than a decade from the modest provision (steeped in socialist and liberal traditions) into a major sector of education—perhaps the largest single area of working-class adult education in the United Kingdom. In doing so, and in sustaining itself under the adverse political regime of the eighties, it has made remarkably few compromises with government or with educational providers—certainly a source of occasional friction with the latter. Its contribution has contained much of profound and lasting educational value. Our survey suggests, however, that educational factors will play only a part in its future.

Union educational debates will reflect debates about the future direction of the movement itself. A few unions see their future primarily as providing efficient services to their members and shifting away from broader views of social or political purpose. Some services are new, providing more job-oriented courses, while others are retaining the original social and political content.

Much will depend on future funding relationships with government—and these are only partly determined by educational considerations. To the surprise of many—considering its general hostility to trade unions—the Conservative government has continued to provide public funds for trade union education since 1979. Yet it has made significant, if small, changes. Apart from allowing expenditure on short courses, the major shift came with the decision from 1983-84 to earmark a section of the public funds for expenditure only on courses specifically endorsed by the employer as relevant to the employer's workplace and likely to be of benefit to good industrial relations or to improved health and safety in that workplace. Further small changes could be more significant: for instance, if some public funds were to be allocated solely for courses involving both shop stewards and managers or supervisors—"joint training" (see Toombs and Creigh, 1983). More radically, a vociferous pressure group on the right of the Conservative Party continues to argue that courses provided by trade unions are inherently biased and can therefore only be justified if they make no call whatever on public funds (Anderson, 1987). At the time of writing (July 1988), however, it seems more likely that the government will redirect some of the funds it currently allocates through the TUC to certain unions outside the TUC.

Union education's partnership with public educational bodies will be influenced by the major structural changes currently under consideration within British education—for instance, for "higher education" and university extramural departments. These promise to increase still further the need to raise substantial fee income from courses—a requirement the TUC may find difficulty in meeting.

References

Anderson, D. "Academies of Union Unrest?" *The Times*, December 9, 1987.
Commission on Industrial Relations (CIR). *Industrial Relations Training*. London: Her Majesty's Stationery Office, 1972.
McIlroy, J. A. "Adult Education and the Role of the Client—The TUC Education Scheme 1929-80." *Studies in the Education of Adults*, 1985a, *17* (1), 33-58.
McIlroy, J. A. "Pedagogy and Politics in Trade Union Education." *Adult Education*, 1985b, *58* (2), 169-174.
Royal Commission on Trade Unions and Employers' Associations. *1965-68 Report*. London: Her Majesty's Stationery Office, 1968.
Toombs, F., and Creigh, S. "Developments in Joint Industrial Relations Training." *Employment Gazette*, December 1983, pp. 510-516.
Trades Union Congress (TUC). *Annual Report*. London: TUC, 1973.
Trades Union Congress (TUC). *Review of the TUC's Education Service*. London: TUC, 1987.
Trades Union Congress (TUC). *Training Shop Stewards*. London: TUC, 1968.

John Holford is tutor/organizer responsible for trade union education with the Workers' Educational Association's southeastern district, UK, and author of Reshaping Labour *(1988).*

Throughout the late 1970s and 1980s, Britain, along with other western European countries, experienced structural unemployment on a large scale. Adult education has responded to this new situation with initiatives that embrace ideas of both vocational and liberal traditions.

Educational Initiatives with the Unemployed

Nicholas Walters

In 1984 the garage where Harry had always worked closed. Harry was redundant. He had been a storeman dealing with customers' enquiries. He was just fifty and lived with his wife and family of four in a small house owned by the local council for which he paid rent. Harry had never achieved much at school, and he left at the first opportunity. He had an interest in mechanics but no qualifications. Harry was devastated and developed a severe depression. He had new jobs, but they were only short lived. Harry developed a major heart complaint and underwent surgery. His world and his expectations are now very restricted, and most of his time is spent at home. He contacted an Educational Advice and Counseling Service for help.

Before the late 1970s, unemployment was not an issue for British social concern, and the popular belief of the time trusted that the post-Beveridge political consensus had defeated the problem (Beveridge, 1967). But by the mid 1970s, world recession, compounded by the oil crisis, fears of hyperinflation, and public sector overborrowing, sounded warnings of an impending structural crisis in the employment market.

Before this crisis, British adult education had been traditionally divided into three sectors:

P. Jarvis (ed.). *Britain: Policy and Practice in Continuing Education.*
New Directions for Continuing Education, no. 40. San Francisco: Jossey-Bass, Winter 1988. 55

1. Higher education, which included universities and the more vocationally oriented polytechnics and colleges of higher education. All were notionally open to everyone able to qualify.

2. Further education, which included technical and vocational education from preapprentice to diploma level, drifing toward specialized vocational awards at degree level.

3. Adult education, which offered a wide spectrum of part-time courses, many nonvocational, largely based on ideas of learning in a society enjoying increased leisure.

Within these three sectors, knowledge was pursued for its own ends and worth was assumed as integral. The traditional professions maintained their higher status. "Success" depended on a concept of a "good education," a "career," or a "good degree." Doctors were more important than computer engineers. Postwar and postcolonial Britain could, it was believed, be administered by students of the classics. The three sectors all supported this assumption.

The crisis of structural unemployment came as a surprise, not least to education. The rapid collapse of career patterns and new, more realistic expectations demanded subtle and persuasive responses from those involved in the education of adults.

Unemployment Data

The nature of unemployment itself makes specific responses problematic. The unemployed are not a homogeneous group; they are not clearly visible, and many definitions are debated. The official criteria on which Central Government statistics are based have been changed some eighteen times since 1979. The standard criterion is based on the concept of those "available for work," but the practical regulation of this means that many fall outside this close definition.

Taylor (1987) suggests that some five million people in Britain would like paid work but cannot find it. This figure needs setting against the Department of Employment's provisional count seasonally adjusted for March 1987 of 3,042,900, a slightly decreasing statistical trend—11.1 percent of the work force. The issue is further clouded, as geographical percentages vary considerably. The Parliamentary constituency of Liverpool Riverside has an official unemployment rate of 29.2 percent, while constituency figures in the southeast of the country can return rates as low as 3.10. This gives rise to the "North/South Divided Nation Debate," but in reality, communities and neighborhoods vary dramatically.

Taking Initiatives

Initiatives are made difficult in terms of identifying target groups. Official designations, either administrative or academic, are problematic.

The unemployed adult is an individual suffering from increased marginalization and isolation, carrying all the stigma of a threatened loss of identity. The demand and need are for a job and for money, two things that education cannot directly offer.

Social agencies are established to respond to immediate need:

1. The Department of Health and Social Security is established to ensure the availability of a modicum of financial public assistance in order to obviate destitution.

2. The Department of Employment is responsible for providing financial payments for adults "available for work." Through the Manpower Services Commission (renamed the Training Commission), it operates a national network of employment agencies based at Job Centers. It is also responsible for providing national programs of training and retraining for unemployed adults (see Chapter Five, this volume).

The government is investing £1.4 billion in a new scheme, employment training, which will amalgamate current Manpower Service Commission activities. The scheme, targeted at eighteen- to twenty-year-olds but open to adults up to fifty years, offers: assessment, counselling, personal action plans, individual placements, and practical and directed training (Fisher, 1986).

It is in this context that educators and trainers are taking initiatives. To do this involves developing new theoretical paradigms, which in turn leads to changes in institutional practice (Smith, 1987). This is true of educational agencies and institutions. The first steps in this process were taken by educators from varying disciplines and academic backgrounds, along the lines of appraisal: "What can we do as educators about this new situation?" The results are of interest in that the potential application can be described in terms of disciplines *and* unemployment (for example, psychology *and* unemployment, sociology *and* unemployment). This kind of study is often related to educational activities *about* employment. "What it is like to be unemployed in Norwich" is an insight of an example into this kind of initiative (Davies, 1986). More radical is the engagement of initiatives that research and develop provision for and with the unemployed.

Here there is a growing number of undertakings (Charnley, 1985). Many are funded by the Department of Employment through the Manpower Services Commission; others, through the Department of Education and Science's REPLAN and PICKUP schemes supported by many others in local education authorities involving Educational Support Grant-funded staff (MacDonald, 1984).

Themes for New Client Groups

Themes of these initiatives have now emerged.

Trawling for New Client Groups. Concentration has been on tools for access, outreach, and targeting new client groups. Besides the traditional emphasis of adult education on publicity, new approaches have been made that employ collaborative institutional accessing, local radio and press, roll-on/roll-off courses, and drop-in courses. This has had a double effect of reestablishing professional contact with differing agencies and attracting new client groups into education by emphasizing accountability of publicly funded bodies to service community needs beyond "teaching what they can teach" (Handy, 1985). Results have shown themselves in the establishment of Educational Advice Centers and extended the work with the Careers Service, which was formerly restricted to school and college leavers. Such work is leading to the description of new curriculum models (Watts, 1985). Targeting has identified groups with shared experience amongst the unemployed, for example; the MSC RESTART initiative for the long-term unemployed and the University of Surrey's work with the early retired are examples from practice. This activity is the result of making direct contact with the unemployed and attempting to assess and respond to educational need.

Job Finding. A second theme relates to job finding. While there is a large gap between the number of unemployed adults and the number of vacancies, a large number of initiatives has been taken that relates to job-finding skills. Currently, the MSC Job Club initiative is most active on this front. The concept behind Job Clubs has been drawn largely from North American experience, and the central object is to help members of the club get the best possible job in the shortest possible time. The value of short-term, intensive job search experience is not universally accepted, and questions are asked about the value of the ethic and its simplisticness. This is exemplified at its crudest in the display of a "Role of Honor"—a public notice of individuals who have found positions. Other initiatives have been successfully targeted at Women Returners in the traditions of the social and life skills movement. Job-finding skills are often an integral part of a wider curriculum for unemployed groups, but many programs concern themselves more with a situation of "no appropriate jobs on offer."

Job Creation. A third theme is that of job creation and self-employment. The Enterprise Allowance Scheme of the MSC offers financial support to new self-employment and small business schemes. Business studies departments are taking a keen interest in training in this field. The interest is supported by an informal national movement of enterprise trusts, often supported by local business communities, offering advice and help from the generation of business ideas to the mechanics of maintaining a small business. Results, judged on a success-or-fail basis, are variable. This option leads to other initiatives in the area of new job creation. The Cooperative Development Association has been established to foster the growth of workers' cooperatives and to support educational programs to promote this model.

By far the largest growth area in job creation has been the Community Program Scheme of the MSC, which offers work opportunities on a temporary basis for the long-term unemployed. Contracts are usually for one year's duration, and many are part time. In February 1987, there were 247,000 adults in this scheme. There was no universal educational component of this scheme, but individual programs incorporate a staff training and development element on which increasing emphasis has been placed.

Training. A fourth theme is reflected in the increasing emphasis put on training. Traditionally, training has been a feature of further education, which is itself increasingly dependent on MSC funding. However, colleges of further education are now responding to the needs of the unemployed: an early and major initiative taken by a college in this sector was the response to the unemployed steel workers in Consett, sequential to the collapse of a major part of the locality's industrial base (Storrie, 1983).

A major feature of vocational education traditionally undertaken by the further education sector has been funded by the Department of Employment rather than by the Department of Education and Science via local education authorities. For education, a significant development is the use of private agencies by the Department of Employment, along with funded training within established colleges. On the positive side, this opens institutions to the community via the marketplace, but this process easily lends itself to the problems of double accountability. Vocationally related education has been expanded into many adult education programs. Initiatives have been taken to provide educational opportunities to overcome "technophobia," which range from open access computing to word-processing skills and the use of computers in businesses (Walters and Turner, 1986). A scheme offered by the MSC as part of the "Action for Jobs" Program was the Job Training Scheme. This was piloted in ten areas; it was run by managing agents who may be private agents or part of the further education sector and was aimed at helping participants update and increase existing occupational skills or giving participants foundation skills in new occupations. This is an avowed training initiative of a mixture of directed training off the job together with the pursuit of open learning. The programs planned to include "standard" elements: (1) personalized assessment and action plan, (2) job-search training, (3) self-employment skills, (4) training in information technology, and (5) training in basic skills.

The scheme was designed for the long-term unemployed and met considerable hostility from trade unions; the interpretation of the pilot statistics are being questioned. The Department of Education and Science's PICKUP program aims at updating those in employment at risk of professional and commercial obsolescence by funding projects intended to update adults working in the professional, industrial, and commercial areas. This involves a wide variety of local and national projects.

Liberal Education Provision. The fifth theme is in the area of nonvocational opportunities for unemployed adults and stretches across and beyond the three sectors of provision. Access to educational opportunities has been a dominant concept, and varying fee remission schemes operate. Some institutions have developed special provision. Most drop-in centers for the unemployed provide some sort of educational group work. Topics range from motorcycle repairs, to fine art, to literacy, to dance. Special provision is focused on centers that are in direct touch with unemployed adults, but local contacts and environments play a key role in the development of this provision. Some networks have produced local directories of opportunities for the unemployed. Those working in this field find a multiplicity of provision and opportunity. Development of consortia, pools of local resources, and appropriate institutional boundary spanning are now well developed. The collaborative provision model is recognized as the most effective. Institutions working in this area have initiated projects targeted at certain groups, for example, ethnic minorities, women, and the younger unemployed. The curriculum is different from mainstream adult education courses in that there is a particular concentration on the individual "in difficulties," and elements of advice, counseling, and personal support are integral to such special programs. Special provision tends to be client led rather than subject based. Some schemes have attempted to establish self-help groups among the unemployed, using tutors who are unemployed themselves. Community groups that rely on voluntary labor have also taken initiatives, such as citizens advice bureaus, churches, and the Workers' Educational Association. Free-standing groups have emerged but more often than not depend in some way on professional resources.

The social life for the unemployed adult is severely curtailed. Mobility is restricted; access to social institutions is often limited. Physical education facilities have been made more available, and campaigning by drop-in centers for the unemployed can result in substantial concessions in both the public and private sector, for example, cinemas, theaters, and swimming pools.

Personal Impacts. The sixth area of work has concentrated on the theme of personal difficulties. The impact of unemployment on the integrity of the individual has had considerable attention. Now, counseling services on a one-to-one basis are being developed. There is a growing consensus concerning the seriousness of the crisis. The impact of unemployment on health, family relationships, personal finance, and law and order concerns are now well documented. The psychological impacts have been well discussed (Berryman, 1984). In response to this, courses are being provided on such topics as Welfare Rights, Healthy Eating, and Survival on a Limited Budget.

Issues for Staff

To support work on these themes, staff training is now a rapidly developing area, both in terms of specialist interest and in local concern. REPLAN gives considerable attention to staff development through its network of regional field officers. Evaluation is problematic and still requires further attention. Success or failure in future employability is clearly simplistic. There is no point in assessing effectiveness in terms of the number in the unemployed register, when neither the educator nor the learner has any control over the availability and quality of vacancies (Walters, 1987). However, it cannot be said that education initiatives concerning the unemployed have nothing to do with employment. Much emphasis is placed by tutors on building self-confidence, self-esteem and self-respect, but this tends to be individual and dependent on societal confidence, which can be misplaced. It is also true that the assumed value of progression paths in an academic sense is insufficient as a criterion. Educators are exploring methods of evaluation that attempt to help both learner and teacher monitor self- and group change (Hobrough, Lawton, and Walters, 1986). Educational initiatives can perhaps be patterned on other professions in order to develop realistic methods (Heiner, 1987).

From these initiatives, issues have evolved. Besides, the sharing of practice by professionals, further debate is continuing in the fields of developing educational theory, educational philosophy, social policy, and personal development. Educators in Britain have produced NEXUS, an unemployment education journal, to forward this topic. National associations have put unemployment on their agendas and now other groups of educators are actively studying the issues involved. There is also a growing awareness that this phenomenon is not peculiar to Britain. Educators in Britain are learning from the experiences of other countries. A Franco/German/British study seminar is currently holding annual meetings in each country. European initiatives have been taken by the National Institute of Adult Continuing Education and the European Bureau of Adult Education, and ongoing consultations about issues, based on practical experience, are now an integral part of the work.

Conclusion

Unemployed adults are unemployed full time for twenty-four hours of the day. This leads to problems about time structures. Time needs to be filled; jobs need to be found and created. Traditional institutional provision is often geared to an eight-hour working day. Initiatives with unemployed adults question such assumptions. In practice, it is no longer appropriate to assume the validity of previously held ideas about career structures. There is little point in offering educational experiences as a pure job substitute at whatever level of academic or professional expertise. Initiatives are taking a wider view as a matter of reality, and this movement is beginning to ask fundamental questions about the control and ownership of the curriculum. In a society that relies on a society policy of consensus about the "success" ethic, there is, by definition, a proportion of the population that is society's failures.

References

Berryman, J. *The Psychological Effects of Unemployment.* Leicester, UK: University of Leicester, 1984.
Beveridge, Lord. *Full Employment in a Free Society.* London: Allan & Unwin, 1967.
Charnley, A. H. *Education for the Adult Unemployed.* London: National Institute of Adult and Continuing Education, 1985.
Davies, M. *What It's Like to Be Unemployed in Norwich.* East Anglia, UK: Welfare Industry Group, University of East Anglia, 1986.
Fisher, H. "Education and Training in a Changing Employment Market in the United Kingdom." *Newsletter* (European Bureau of Adult Education, The Netherlands), 1986.
Handy, C. *The Future of Work.* Oxford, UK: Blackwell, 1985.
Heiner, M. *Evaluation Sozialer Arbeit: Auf de Suche nach neuen Konzepten"* [Evaluation of social work: Toward the search for new concepts]. Bonn: Theorie und Praxis der Socialen Arbeit, 1987.
Hobrough, J., Lawton, E., and Walters, N. *New Strategies in Outreach and Access: A Feasibility Study.* Guildford, UK: Department of Educational Studies, University of Surrey, 1986.
MacDonald, J. *Education for Unemployed Adults.* London: Department of Education and Science, 1984.
Smith, G. "The Great Debate." *NEXUS*, 1987, *1*.
Storrie, T. *Conset.* London: Further Education Unit, 1983.
Taylor, D. *Forceful Arguments.* London: Unemployment Unit, 1987.
Walters, N., and Turner, M. *Office Technology.* Guildford, UK: Guildford Area Unemployed Peoples Centre, University of Surrey, 1986.
Walters, N. "Legitimate Hope in Unemployment Education." *NEXUS*, 1987, *1*, 24-28.
Watts, A. *Adult Unemployment and the Curriculum.* London: F.E.U./Replan, 1985.

Nicholas Walters is staff tutor in educational studies at the University of Surrey, UK, and is responsible for community education programs at the Guildford Institute of the University of Surrey.

Professional bodies are the moving force behind the expansion of continuing professional education in the United Kingdom.

Developments in Continuing Education in the Professions

Linda Welsh

Much of the information in this chapter comes from research recently undertaken for the Further Education Unit and PICKUP in the Department of Education and Science, including the case studies in the concluding section. Medicine and education were omitted because they have comparatively well-researched and well-funded continuing education systems.

The study was undertaken largely in response to the apparent increase in interest in continuing education, or more specifically, in continuing professional development over recent years among professional bodies. A questionnaire survey was undertaken early in 1987, and 123 out of some 200 professional bodies responded. In addition, much written material was reviewed, and five detailed case studies were undertaken. Detailed information was also made available from two further professional bodies.

Developing the Educational Role

A traditional role of professional bodies is to set standards of knowledge and competence for entrants to the professions. About half of the responding professional bodies operate an examination system to assess entrants, indicating that professional bodies are active in maintaining *direct* control over educational standards of new members. Over half of the respondent bodies operate a system of recognizing graduate courses run by further and higher educational institutions that allow full exemption from the professional bodies' own examinations.

Some bodies operate both systems at the same time, although there is a trend toward recognizing courses run by educational institutions and dropping examinations run by the professional bodies. Even where direct control over educational standards has been delegated to educational institutions, the professional bodies operate systems for monitoring the standards of courses, and thereby the educational qualifications of new entrants.

As this traditional educational role has developed and systems have improved to handle initial standards, interest has developed in continuing standards of competence. Nearly half of the respondents to the survey have policies on continuing education or continuing professional development (CPD), with a further one-third in the process of considering introducing CPD policies. As yet, only a small minority (6 percent) have compulsory CPD, and one-fifth set minimum amounts of CPD in their schemes.

Terminology

Already, two terms have been used to describe the process by which professionals maintain and improve their professional competence, namely *continuing education* and *continuing professional development*. There is a proliferation of terms used to describe this activity, which inevitably leads to misunderstanding. For example, the engineering professions use *continuing education and training* (CET), lawyers use two terms, *postqualifying legal education* (PQLE) and *continuing professional development* (CPD), and the majority of the construction professions use *continuing professional development* (CPD).

Even where the same term is used, it may not refer to the same activity. For example, lawyers use CPD for that educational activity that is required by new members to achieve their practice certificate, while surveyors use CPD to refer to all activity undertaken by practicing members to maintain their professional competence.

The term enjoying most favor is *continuing professional development* (CPD); increasingly, it is being adopted by professional bodies. In this study the term *continuing education* (CE) will be used and should be read as being the same as CPD. In this chapter, CE refers to: the systematic maintenance, improvement, and broadening of knowledge and skills and the development of personal qualities necessary for the execution of professional and technical duties throughout the practitioner's working life. This is a definition adopted by the U.K. CPD in Construction Group.

Rationale for the Emerging CE Role of Professional Bodies

Although involvement in CE is facilitated by delegation of direct control over initial education, which then frees professional body staff to progress to other initiatives, such as continuing education, delegation is not a prerequisite for professional bodies being concerned with and active in CE. The aim of CE is to help members maintain professional competence and thereby the quality of professional services.

The key motivations for developing CE policies and schemes or programs come from a variety of sources. The case studies and other information point to client influence being important in promoting concern with CE. Increasingly, high standards of professional competence are demanded by clients, as evidenced by complaints to professional bodies and the amount of litigation against individual professionals and firms. Professional bodies often have obligations to the public regarding the standards of professional services offered to clients. For example, the Royal Charter of the Royal Town Planning Institute specifically states that the object of the institute is to "advance the science and art of Town Planning . . . for the benefit of the public, and for that purpose . . . shall have the power to . . . ensure that corporate membership . . . shall be open only to those competent to engage in Town Planning" (RTPI, 1987). Other professional bodies that do not have such detailed objectives in their Royal Charter are also active in promoting CE among their membership.

Employers expect their professional staff to be competent, and it is in the interest of professional bodies to promote CE among members to assist continuing competence and thereby maintain the confidence in their qualifications and membership. Thus the public image of the profession motivates toward developing CE policy and practice, and this action is not always taken in response to criticism but from a sense of pride in the profession.

Another key motivation is the amount and speed of change in knowledge and practice within a profession. Initial vocational degree courses are reckoned by some to have a useful life of only two to three years. Job satisfaction can also be improved by CE, and some professional bodies are aware of this in their promotion of CE. Due to the increase of certain vocational degree courses in the early 1960s, there is evidence of a bulge in several professions in the thirty-five to fifty age group, which can limit promotion opportunities. CE can help professionals cope with current work better, prepare for promotion, or prepare for a change of job.

Who Is Responsible for Continuing Education for Professionals?

This a controversial question to which there are a variety of responses. Opinions are many, and often views are strongly held. Responsibility can be taken narrowly in the sense of "who pays," but it is also usually a matter of attitude and commitment to action. Central government holds the view that training/CE should be self-financing, although there is much support through various departmental initiatives and educational institutions.

Employers have a responsibility to their clients to provide a competent and efficient professional service, and many do have staff development programs designed to improve their staff's professional ability. However, there is much concern over the low level of investment in training at all levels in the majority of British firms, and it is not uncommon for professionals to undertake CE without any support from their employers.

It is a characteristic of many professions that members work either in small firms or work in small groups within larger firms. Small firms, on average, seem to spend less on training/CE than the larger firms, and CE is not commonly viewed as an investment, but as a cost.

Individual professionals have responsibility for their own competence and a right and duty to undertake CE. However, it is argued that CE for professionals is a shared responsibility between the individual, the professional bodies, and the employers. Individuals ignore their responsibilities at the risk of losing their jobs or not gaining promotion. Employers ignore their responsibilities at the risk of being less competitive, losing clients, and having legal action taken against them for negligence or incompetence. Staff development is a management responsibility that is often neglected.

In promoting CE policies and schemes, professional bodies can assist individual members and their employers to achieve competence and maintain their relevance and worth to the profession and the public.

CE Policy and Practice

Having briefly reviewed why professional bodies are or should be concerned with CE, let us turn to the response to the questionnaire survey for information on what action is being taken on CE by the professional bodies. The goal of CE is to help maintain competence, and half the respondents have codes of professional conduct that mention maintaining or improving competence.

Nearly half have CE policies, and a further 31 percent are considering introducing a CE policy. This is either in response to guidelines set by influential bodies, such as the Engineering Council, or as member initiatives.

Some professional bodies set very specific objectives for their CE schemes, for example one-fifth set minimum quantities of CE, albeit fairly modest amounts. The Law Society sets specific targets, with obligatory topics, which must be met by all newly qualified solicitors.

Only a small number of respondents, seven, have compulsory CE. Again there is confusion over terminology, as there is no consensus on the frequently used terms *compulsory, obligatory, mandatory, required,* or *voluntary*, all of which are used in relation to CE in the professional bodies. The only truly mandatory CE scheme is for midwives who have a statutory CE obligation.

Only twenty-two bodies issue CE record cards, of which only half require that these are returned to headquarters for monitoring purposes. Monitoring can also be undertaken in other ways, for example, through sample survey and direct feedback from members. As many professional bodies have limited resources, it is understandable at this early stage in development that scarce resources are primarily directed at promotion of CE and improving available opportunities.

Some institutes have undertaken pilot schemes and other research to help gain systematic information to decide on future CE policy and practice. For example, physiotherapists have consulted widely among the membership on policies and strategies for postregistration education and have researched (and continue to research) a range of relevant issues. Much effort has been devoted to identifying needs and attempting to develop provisions to meet these needs, rather than setting up systems of control or sanction.

The importance attached to CE can be seen in CE staff figures: 60 percent of respondent bodies have paid staff engaged in CE activities. The number of staff range from one to fourteen, with the majority having only one or two CE staff. Their main areas of work are in organizing events, dealing with administrative matters (such as the CE budgets), and preparing distance learning materials. A small number of professional bodies have staff involved in CE policy and development work rather than administrative work.

Over one-third of respondents have specific CE budget allocations (excluding staff), ranging from £500 to over £1 million (taking account of proceeds from conferences and other events), and a further 30 percent are considering committing funds to CE in the future. There needs to be caution in drawing conclusions from these statistics, as much more detailed information is needed on what is included in budgets and what is defined as CE in different professional bodies. For example, in a number of institutes, much of CE work and activities is carried out by branches and therefore is not always included under a CE budget heading. In some professional bodies, CE events offer an important source of revenue, and much effort is devoted to organizing programs of conferences and similar events.

Over one-third of responding professional bodies have made systematic attempts to assess CE needs at headquarters and/or branch level. A further one-fourth are considering such research in the future. Information from these surveys is useful in improving the CE opportunities available to ensure that they meet the needs expressed.

Nearly two-thirds of respondents liaise at headquarters with educational institutions to ensure the CE provided by them is relevant and appropriate. There is further liaison operating at branch level in about one-third of responding professional bodies. Often, such formal liaison is strengthened by informal links, for example, academic staff being members of local branches' committees of professional bodies. Liaison with other providers in these ways can improve local and national CE provision.

Some CE needs cannot be met by center-based learning opportunities, whether offered by the professional bodies, educational institutions, or other providers. CE by other means also needs to be promoted—for example, distance learning, office-based learning, job exchanges, and systematic home reading. Studies, such as the CEM study among surveyors, show the importance of informal CE through home study.

Emerging Trends

Many, if not most, of the professional bodies have been active in developing CE policies and strategies only in the last decade, with an notable increase in the last five years.

With over three-quarters of respondent bodies having a CE policy, or considering introducing a CE policy, it is clear that CE for members is an important concern for professional bodies. Cyril Houle (1984) has stated that "often [continuing education] subsequently became the chief responsibility of the bureaucracy which maintained the organized profession" (p. 191).

Strategies vary, and there seem to be two major trends. First, there is a move toward mandatory CE schemes, as evidenced in the Royal Institute of British Architects, the Law Society, the Incorporated Society of Valuers and Auctioneers, and the Royal Institution of Chartered Surveyors. Second, there is a move toward schemes that, by and large, are self-assessed and self-determined by individual members, with the professional bodies taking a supportive and encouraging role. This is the route currently being taken by the Royal Town Planning Institute, the Institution of Structural Engineers, the Chartered Society of Physiotherapists, and the Institute of Housing. The aim of both types of strategy is to increase CE provision and take-up rates in order to help members maintain and improve their professional competence.

Case Studies of CE Practice

The Royal Institution of British Architects (RIBA) has been active in promoting CE among the membership (approximately 22,500 practicing members) for several years and was considered by many to be in the vanguard of CE policy and practice by other professions in the construction industry. In 1983 the Education and Professional Development Committee, at the request of the Continuing Professional Development Subcommittee, sought and obtained approval from the council to establish a fund for three of four years from which regional CE pilot schemes could be supported.

Each year, regions (branches) were invited to bid for funds, and over the years 1984, 1985, and 1986, £77,500 was granted for regional CE and a further £12,500 in 1987—£90,000 in total. Eleven regions (out of thirteen) have benefited, and a variety of approaches was adopted, although most included some mechanism for identifying CE needs and running workshops or other CE events.

All these projects were required to submit reports in order to assess the usefulness and transferability of the various approaches, and this has allowed the RIBA to build up a valuable store of knowledge. This in turn lead to the following recommendations to the council in July 1987:
- The introduction of a rolling program of funding for regional CE over five years, followed by a permanent budget allocation to the regional CE service
- A declaration by the council that after 1992 a commitment to a personal CE program will be a requirement for membership
- That the Education and Professional Development Committee should be asked to undertake various activities in support of CE, such as mounting a national awareness campaign, preparing a central data base, and supporting training for CE personnel.

These were all approved. This builds on a general trend within RIBA of devolving resources to the regions.

At the same time, RIBA together with the Barlett School of Architecture have received funding and other supporting services from the Manpower Services Commission and the Construction Industry Training Board for an ambitious open learning project called "Professional Studies in British Architectural Practice." This project involves the production of some 320 learning packages associated with sixteen topic areas arranged into four development phases over three years. These packages are designed for a variety of users and can be used in a variety of ways, such as for individual study or linked to form the basis of longer-term programs of study leading to a postgraduate award.

However, an institute need not be large and relatively rich in resources to make an impact. The Incorporated Society of Valuers and Auctioneers (ISVA) has only 4,626 corporate members and in October 1986 decided to introduce compulsory CE for all members from October 1989. The requirement is not less than twenty hours of structured learning per annum. This to some extent follows developments in the much larger Royal Institution of Chartered Surveyors.

This is a member-initiated scheme and is to be self-validated. Guidance notes will be issued to the thirty-one branches, that are active in running evening professional meetings and other local events often in collaboration with related professional bodies. Provision of CE also comes from headquarters and educational institutions and commercial providers. Headquarters aims to increase provision in the branches and encourage closer links with the educational institutions.

From 1989, members are likely to be required to indicate that CE they have undertaken when returning their annual subscription and professional indemnity insurance notice. Spot checks will be undertaken by headquarters to monitor those who have joined since 1984, but there will be no formal requirement to return ISVA CPD record cards on an annual basis.

Conclusion

CE is still very much in the early stages of development in the professional bodies in the United Kingdom. Significant progress has been made in developing both policies and strategies in many such bodies, more usually in the larger ones. However, there are constraints to progress that should not be understated. The Royal Town Planning Institute (RTPI) identified the following issues at the end of their three-year experimental CE scheme in 1987:

• CE is not fully understood by a significant number of members and employers. Returned CPD record sheets showed many members unclear as to what to include, and hardly any "on the job" CE was evident in returns.

• There are still difficulties in identifying CE needs of individuals and their employers and specifying these to providers. Too often, the test is by explicit demand, and if a course is fully booked, it is judged successful.

• There is a problem of the nonjoiners (or "sleepers," as they are termed in the RIBA). This is largely due to (1) individuals having no incentive to undertake CE and (2) individuals willing to do CE but unable to do so for a variety of reasons.

- There is a need for regular and systematic information on CE opportunities and improved distribution and communication of this information.
- Individuals' difficulties in undertaking CE are exacerbated by employers'/managers' lack of support. Often, even with an enlightened employer, it is still only immediate needs that are catered to, and CE is not undertaken on a systematic basis geared to meet needs.
- CE provision is not adequate in terms of access, topics, quantity, quality, and appropriateness to the particular needs of the practitioner. Too much emphasis is given to events rather than other more flexible modes of learning activity.
- Action is postponed or avoided by trying to pass the responsibility to others.

Professional bodies are in a unique position to promote CE, and the evidence from the survey, limited though it is, shows that many are taking an active and responsible role. Much still needs to be done, and with limited resources, it is important that knowledge and experience is shared as widely as possible to assist progress across the professional boundaries. This is the aim of the CPD in Construction Group and it is hoped that other groupings will develop at local and national levels to assist this process.

References

Houle, C. "Overview of Continuing Professional Education." In Sinclair Goodlad (ed.), *Education for the Professions*. Guildford, UK: SRHE and NFER, University of Surrey, 1984.
Royal Town Planning Institute (RTPI). "Continuing Professional Development." London: RTPI, 1987.

Linda Welsh is a free-lance consultant on continuing professional development (CPD) and is currently engaged in working with the Royal Town Planning Institute, UK, on developing their CPD strategy and advising on government-sponsored research on CPD in the construction industry.

Open learning offers both a coherent methodology and an adaptable range of practical techniques for developing continuing education.

Open Learning and Continuing Education

Malcolm Tight

Philosophy

Continuing education is frequently defined simply in terms of the age and previous educational experience of its participants, though reference is sometimes made to the subject of study and its vocational orientation. But continuing education may (and arguably should) also aim to be distinctive in its approach to the whole process of learning. Open learning is a concept that offers a general form and philosophy that, although it has wider relevance, is particularly appropriate to the education of adults. It is, therefore, well suited for providing a methodological basis for continuing education.

Open learning was recently defined as follows:

> Open learning is a term used to describe courses flexibly designed to meet individual requirements. It is often applied to provision which tries to remove barriers that prevent attendances at more traditional courses, but it also suggests a learner-centered philosophy. Open-learning courses may be offered in a learning center of some kind, or most of the activity may be carried out away from such a center (e.g. at home). In nearly every case specially prepared or adapted materials are necessary [Lewis and Spencer, 1986, pp. 9-10].

It can be seen from this definition that there are a number of aspects to the concept:
- Open learning is designed to be *flexible* in terms of the time, place, and pace of study.
- Open learning seeks to be *learner centered*, tailoring provision to meet the needs of particular individuals or groups of learners.
- Open learning is concerned with the *removal of barriers* preventing access to learning opportunities, including institutional, attitudinal, and financial barriers.
- Open learning typically involves the use of *learning materials* (often referred to as learning "packs" or "packages") in addition to, or instead of, classroom instruction.
- Open learning may be *based anywhere:* in an educational institution, a factory, a local community center, or in the home.

Using this schema, learning opportunities can be visualized as ranging along a spectrum between ideal "open" and "closed" forms. Any particular example will usually incorporate a mix of relatively open and relatively closed elements (Lewis, 1986).

Clearly, open learning is closely related to—but by no means synonymous with—a number of other concepts that have gained increasingly wide acceptance in recent years. Open learning initiatives typically make use of *distance education* techniques, but can be applied without them, while distance educators need not adopt an open learning approach. Similarly, open learning will usually apply appropriate *educational technology*, but these facilities may be employed as part of any teaching or learning strategy. And, though open learning will normally involve a considerable amount of *independent learning*, and will also make use of *experiential learning*, it seldom relies entirely on these means.

Practice

Open learning has had an increasing impact on educational and training practices in the United Kingdom. Over the last two decades, the concept has been seized on and developed through a succession of national and local initiatives. Open learning is a powerful slogan, and it is not surprising that it has sometimes been interpreted in different ways by different interests, or that there has been some reinvention of the wheel along the way (MacKenzie, Postgate, and Scupham, 1975). Indeed, many educational providers now practice at least some of the principles of open learning without explicitly labeling it as such, and some of them had been doing so long before the concept was in general use.

The Open University is, without doubt, the best-known British example of open learning practice. Established in 1969, it has steadily expanded its range of undergraduate, postgraduate, and postexperience courses and now has over 80,000 students studying for credit at a distance (with a similar number taking short courses). Its effective use of a large-scale, high-quality (and expensive) multimedia teaching system—incorporating specially prepared instructional texts, broadcast television and radio programs, audio and videocassettes, home experiment kits, tutorials, and summer schools—has inspired development and imitation at all levels of educational provision both in Britain and worldwide (Perry, 1976; Thorpe and Grugeon, 1987). Yet, as far as the bulk of its undergraduate and postgraduate provision is concerned, while the Open University embodies many of the elements of open learning, it compromises on or ignores others.

The Open University is open to all comers, whatever their age or educational background, and students may be based anywhere in the United Kingdom, provided that they are prepared to wait for a place if necessary. Some help with fees is possible in hardship cases, and courses may be taken one after another in virtually any combination over an indefinite period to make up a degree. But neither the curriculum nor its method of delivery is particularly flexible. Courses are only provided in certain academic subjects, and it is only possible to commence study at one time during the year. If students wish to successfully complete courses and gain credits, they must accept a rigid timetable and structure for reading, assignment submission, and examination.

Of course, much the same observations may be made about the various private and correspondence colleges that have, for many years, provided instruction for a range of professional qualifications and certificates. Despite the innovations it has introduced in teaching methods, therefore, the Open University should be seen as following closely in their tradition.

The other major British provider of open learning opportunities for adults at undergraduate and postgraduate level, the University of London External Degree System, is less well known. Yet this system has enabled students to prepare for degree examinations anywhere in the world, solely by private study, ever since 1858 (Tight, 1987b). It currently has around 25,000 registered students, slightly more than half of them based in Britain. Until recently, the University itself did not offer these students any teaching facilities, though correspondence colleges and other institutions have provided courses in some subjects. An "independent guided study" system is now being introduced by the University, however, invoving short courses, practice examinations, and advice sessions. Compared to the Open University, the External System is more open in terms of the study patterns available to students, though it remains less open in setting entry requirements.

A third major operator in the open learning field, the National

Extension College (NEC), has close links with both the Open University and the London External Degree System, acting in many ways as a precursor for the former while continuing to arrange tutorial support for the latter's students (Freeman, 1983). However, its major contribution in this area has been the development, in conjunction with Barnet College and others, of "flexistudy" for further education students (Barnet College, 1980; Sacks, 1980). This scheme, using NEC-produced learning materials and local college teaching staff and facilities, combines home study with occasional face-to-face tutorials, allowing for continuous enrollment, learning at the student's own pace, and the pursuit of special interests.

During the late 1970s and early 1980s, many institutions of further and higher education began to extend their provision for nontraditional students and in doing so applied some of the principles underlying open learning. These initiatives varied widely in both scope and success, ranging from a willingness to allow students to sit in on parts of existing courses to the design of new types of courses specifically for certain adult groups. A good example of the latter approach is the independent studies program created at North East London Polytechnic. This enables students to draw up their own study programs and methods of assessment for degree courses and then pursue them by either full-time or part-time study (Stephenson, 1983).

The open colleges movement (not to be confused with the more recent Open College) dates from the same period. Its concern is with preparing nontraditional students for entry to higher or further education, though open college or "access" courses are frequently also pursued as an end in themselves. The first such "college," the Open College of the North West (OCNW), was established in 1976, based at the University of Lancaster, Preston (now Lancashire) Polytechnic and several local colleges. It offers a broad curriculum of study skills and interdisciplinary learning, designed as an adult alternative to certification (Percy and Lucas, 1980). The OCNW currently enrolls thousands of students each year, though relatively few have so far gone on to degree study.

There are now open colleges or access courses available in many parts of the country: nearly 100 institutions were identified as offering such courses in England alone in 1985, mainly on a part-time basis (Lucas and Ward, 1985). In some cases, the curriculum can be negotiated, courses are available on a number of local sites or at a distance, and study may be pursued at different paces. Other courses are less flexible and may be linked to a specific degree intake. Formal entry qualifications are, as with the Open University, not required, and course fees are usually kept low (Davies and Robertson, 1986). Though the impact of the open colleges movement on conventional higher education has, to date, been slight, with national policy moving toward increased access, it is likely to become more influential in the future, particularly as regards part-time higher education (Tight, 1987a).

Application to Vocational Education

In the last few years, the application of open learning techniques to vocational continuing education has become much more prominent, as both private and public sector employers, encouraged by the government, have come to accept the practical benefits. Using open learning formats, it is possible, for example, for employees to study prepared materials by themselves or in groups during slack time, or their own time, with the materials retained and updated for further use by others. A great deal of the impetus for these developments has come from the Manpower Services Commission (MSC), a central government agency that, through its National Training Initiative, has steadily been extending its influence from further education for adolescents to continuing education for adults.

The Open Tech was set up under the MSC's umbrella in 1982 to oversee and make available "pump-priming" funds for collaborative, developmental, open learning projects at technician and supervisory levels (MSC, 1982). Though the Open Tech program as such only lasted for a few years, its role has now been assumed by an Open Learning Unit within the MSC. The numerous schemes it has helped to get off the ground have varied from learning packages for workers in amenity horticulture to interactive videos on handling hazardous materials to teleconferencing systems for management (NEC, 1986). Some of these ventures subsequently proved unable to fund themselves and folded once the initial development period was over. Others have proved more successful and have added to the growing array of open learning activities supported by employers, professional bodies, and employees.

Some of these activities are provided directly by employers themselves on their own premises, while others are arranged by educational institutions. In the latter case, they are frequently organized by an open learning unit within the college concerned. Such units typically offer a range of vocational and nonvocational provision and may be involved in initial as well as continuing education. They may, for example, provide flexistudy courses for school and further education certificates alongside updating packages for technicians and managers (Bagley and Challis, 1985; Scottish Education Department, 1982; Spencer, 1980). The degree of flexibility and openness of these opportunities varies considerably. Though learning packages tend to be designed on the premise that they can be studied anywhere, at any time, and at any pace (unless they require the use of specialized equipment), other "open learning" courses may be intended for a limited audience and not made generally available.

The principles of open learning are now being extended to higher-level postexperience vocational provision in universities, polytechnics, and colleges of higher education, with the PICKUP program sponsored by the Department of Education and Science acting as a catalyst. In many ways analogous to the MSC's Open Tech initiative, PICKUP has made available "pump-priming" funds for the organization, provision, and marketing of short updating courses for the professions, industry, and commerce. Not all of this provision is open learning, but much is, and most major institutions of higher education are now involved. The Open University has been a pioneer in this area as well, with its Open Business School now claiming to be the largest in Western Europe. Other universities have taken the opportunity provided by PICKUP to build on their existing—usually fairly limited—provision of vocational continuing education. In the process, continuing education has frequently been accorded a much more central location within the institutional structure and policy.

The Open College

The most recent development of all in this field, the Open College, got under way in September 1987 after barely a year's planning (Open College, 1987). With only a small core staff and limited funding, this is essentially an exercise in adapting and building on existing resources, including Open Tech and NEC materials. The Open College will make use of television broadcasts, learning packages, and a national network of advisory and referral points. Its eventual audience is visualized in millions, consisting of actual and potential supervisor staff, managers, and technicians—both employed and unemployed—who wish to upgrade or develop their skills. Course provision will range from basic numeracy to subdegree-level study: there will be no entrance requirements, and fees will be varied according to students' ability to pay. If it is successful, the Open College cannot but have an enormous impact on the whole British educational system, creating as well as recognizing demands and expectations and establishing the ideology of open learning firmly in the public mind.

Problems

All of the initiatives outlined here together comprise a sizable and expanding sector of continuing education. As has been indicated, the characteristics of this provision, and the nature and extent of the openness practiced, varies a great deal. In some cases, open learning schemes have been adopted primarily because of their cost-effectiveness and flexibility (these two factors are obviously closely related), rather than because of their potential educational benefits as such. This in itself suggests some of the disadvantages associated with the application of conventional teaching and training methods to continuing education.

Open learning is, naturally, not without its own drawbacks (or challenges), though a number of these relate to the context in which it is provided rather than to the provision itself. There may, for example, be considerable opposition to the introduction of open learning inside companies or educational institutions that have traditionally offered other forms of education or training (Elton, 1987; Further Education Unit, 1983). It is not surprising then that many of the more successful open learning initiatives—and certainly the most visible—have either involved the creation of wholly new institutions, such as the Open University, or have relied on well-publicized national initiatives to draw on and restructure existing provision and enthusiasm throughout the country, as in the case of the Open Tech and PICKUP. Where open learning units are established in existing organizations, the firm commitment of top-level management is obviously of critical importance for their survival and subsequent success.

When the decision has been taken to develop open learning, a series of practical management problems then quickly become apparent. Decisions on demand and marketing; the aims and objectives of provision; the media to be employed; the preparation and/or adaptation of learning materials; the scheduling of production and distribution, evaluation, and quality control; and funding, costing, and pricing all require careful consideration. Fortunately, there is now considerable expertise available to draw on in many of these areas (Bates, 1984; Birch and Latham, 1984; Rumble, 1986).

In addition, there are issues associated with the staffing of open learning schemes: selection, training, motivation, and reward. These are particularly relevant in cases where staff employed in conventional education or training are being engaged to produce or support open learning materials, since experience indicates that teachers, lecturers, trainers, and administrators are seldom as adaptable as might be expected or desired. The skills required by open learning are very different from those used in classroom instruction, and it is not usual to find them in the same people. Open learning really has more in common with publishing than with school.

Finally, there may be difficulties with clients, whether these are individual students or companies. Many of these problems—enrollment, support, retention, assessment—are also encountered in other forms of education or training, though they will be interpreted in rather different ways. Open learning users need to be supported in ways that enable them to use learning packages as they want, and not necessarily as those who compiled the materials originally envisaged. Students may be examined during or at the end of their studies, but only where this is deemed relevant or desirable by those involved. And, where materials are intended for flexible use, this may not be sequential or complete, and students will opt to finish their studies at different stages for positive and perfectly valid reasons.

Prospects

Open learning is now a permanent part of the British education and training scene. Its methods are being applied in all sectors, at all levels, and to all types of provision, with considerable success. But it is particularly relevant for adults, who appreciate its flexibility and are better able to utilize the freedom and responsibility it gives them to determine the how, when, where, and what of *their* learning. Open learning is also well suited to short, highly specific forms of study, so its impact is always likely to be greatest in continuing education applications.

Indeed, it may be argued that continuing education, and especially postexperience vocational provision, has been waiting for open learning to enable it to take off in a big way. Open learning might well have been—perhaps it was—invented to meet this need.

References

Bagley, B., and Challis, B. *The Experience of Open Learning.* London: Further Education Unit, 1985.
Barnet College of Further Education. *Flexistudy: A Manual for Local Colleges.* Cambridge, UK: National Extension College, 1980.
Bates, A. (ed.). *The Role of Technology in Distance Education.* London: Croom Helm, 1984.
Birch, D., and Latham, J. *Managing Open Learning.* London: Further Education Unit, 1984.
Davies, D., and Robertson, D. "Open College: Towards a New View of Adult Education." *Adult Education,* 1986, *59* (2), 106-114.
Elton, L. *Teaching in Higher Education: Appraisal and Training.* London: Kogan Page, 1987.
Freeman, R. "The National Extension College." In M. Tight (ed.), *Educational Opportunities for Adults.* London: Croom Helm, 1983.
Further Education Unit. *Flexible Learning Opportunities.* London: Further Education Unit, 1983.
Lewis, R. "What Is Open Learning?" *Open Learning,* 1986, *1* (2), 5-10.
Lewis, R., and Spencer, D. *What Is Open Learning?* London: Centre for Educational Technology, 1986.
Lucas, S., and Ward, P. (eds.). *A Survey of "Access" Courses in England.* Lancaster, UK: University of Lancaster School of Education, 1985.

MacKenzie, N., Postgate, R., and Scupham, J. *Open Learning: Systems and Problems in Post-secondary Education.* Paris: UNESCO Press, 1975.

Manpower Services Commission (MSC). *Open Tech Task Group Report.* Sheffield, UK: Manpower Services Commission, 1982.

National Extension College (NEC). *Open Tech Directory.* Cambridge, UK: National Extension College, 1986.

Open College. *The Opening College.* London: Open College, 1987.

Percy, K., and Lucas, S. (eds.). *The Open College and Alternatives.* Lancaster, UK: University of Lancaster, 1980.

Perry, W. *Open University: A Personal Account by the First Vice-Chancellor.* Milton Keynes, UK: Open University Press, 1976.

Rumble, G. *The Planning and Management of Distance Education.* London: Croom Helm, 1986.

Sacks, H. "Flexistudy: An Open Learning System for Further and Adult Education." *British Journal of Educational Technology,* 1980, *11* (2), 85-95.

Scottish Education Department. *Distance No Object: Examples of Open Learning in Scotland.* Edinburgh: Her Majesty's Stationery Office, 1982.

Spencer, D. *Thinking about Open Learning Systems.* London: Council for Educational Technology, 1980.

Stephenson, J. "Higher Education: School for Independent Study." In M. Tight (ed.), *Adult Learning and Education.* London: Croom Helm, 1983.

Thorpe, M., and Grugeon, D. (eds.). *Open Learning for Adults.* Harlow, UK: Longmans, 1987.

Tight, M. "Access and Part-time Undergraduate Study." *Journal of Access Studies,* 1987a, *2* (1), 12-24.

Tight, M. "London University External Developments." *Open Learning,* 1987b, *2* (2), 49-51.

Malcolm Tight is director of the unit for research into part-time higher education at Birkbeck College, University of London, UK.

This chapter examines the plight of general education and concludes with a model of society and the place of education within it which appear to underlie the thoughts of the policymakers.

The Future of Continuing Education

Peter Jarvis

Traditionally, there has been a distinction drawn between vocational and nonvocational education that has led to some rather sterile debates about the nature of education and the extent to which so-called nonvocational education actually had vocational usages, and vice versa. Consequently, it was not surprising that the Advisory Council for Adult and Continuing Education (ACACE, 1979) sought to abolish this distinction by proposing that within continuing education, two forms of education should be recognized: those of vocational and general education. The former was regarded as specifically related to occupation, while the latter was broader and more general. The council went on to specify that the purpose of the course was more significant in its classification than the actual content. However, two forms of education still remained within the broader framework of continuing education, and this was to become significant in the following years.

It was pointed out in the opening chapter that within the framework of continuing education proposed for universities, extramural education was retained. Indeed, the universities have, in a variety of ways, provided a general extramural educational service in the United Kingdom since the autumn of 1867, when James Stuart delivered what is generally regarded as the first series of extramural classes (Kelly, 1970, pp. 219ff.). However, in the twentieth century, it was not only the universities but the Workers' Education Association, the local education authorities, and a variety of other organizations that all offered general education for the local population. Indeed, it was laid upon the local education authorities in the 1944 Education Act to provide a comprehensive educational service. The actual wording of the act was cited in the first chapter, and need not be repeated here.

However, conditions have altered since that famous act was passed, and governmental attitudes have changed and hardened. This chapter briefly traces some of these changes in the first section and, in the second, seeks to construct a model of society and locate education within it that reflects the present policy decisions. Finally, while predictions about the future are not the objective of this exercise, a few thoughts about the way that education will develop in the short term in the United Kingdom are offered.

The Future of General Education

It will have become clear that in recent years, considerable finance has been made available to the vocational element in continuing education, as most of the foregoing chapters in this volume have demonstrated. Much of this finance has been for short-term projects, often of a "pump-priming" nature. However, the same cannot be claimed for the adult general form of continuing education.

Traditionally, the government has made grants to universities and the Workers' Educational Association (WEA), as "responsible bodies," to provide general education of a university standard in the community and for the WEA to continue its work with the trade unions. Additionally, the government has made grants to local authorities to carry out all their educational responsibilities within their locality, including that of providing adult education within the area. The provision of education has included that of further, or general, continuing education as defined by the 1944 act. However, it is necessary to trace briefly the changes that have taken place in order to see clearly the trends that have been occurring.

University extramural provision has normally been regarded as having three sources of funding: three-quarters of the basic cost directly funded from the Department of Education and Science; one-quarter funded by the local university from its own income from the University Grants Commission; and, in addition, the fee income from those who enrolled in courses. However, the courses offered had to be completely open, so that any member of the public could enroll for any course. This restricted the types of courses that could be offered, since certain vocational courses were ruled out as not being totally open. However, changes began to happen in the early 1980s. Initially, the formula for funding was changed, which naturally resulted in less direct income and the need to increase fee income. This resulted in dramatic increases in fees for courses, which in turn restricted the potential clientele for extramural courses to those who could afford the level of fee being asked. The monies withdrawn were offered back to the universities in the form of short-term grants for innovative projects in extramural provision. Gradually, however, the concept of openness was also eroded, so that it became possible to offer courses of a vocational nature under the "responsible body" extramural provision.

In addition, universities and polytechnics have been encouraged in recent years to establish a continuing education program, as Chapter Three shows, and a great deal of effort and finance has gone into establishing this. If universities and polytechnics were not themselves receiving severe financial cuts, it would have been possible for them to continue to develop both aspects of the continuing education program. But because finance is not available, the general adult education program has suffered in the process.

Local authority adult education has fared no better. As early as 1980, it was being suggested that there was need for an economic adult education service, which was taken to mean that there were about to be cuts in the grant from central government. The decision to decrease the grant to local authorities still gave them autonomy to inflict the financial cuts wherever they so wished within their provision of services—whether it be the social services, the library services, education, or even refuse collections! Later in 1980, the Department of Education and Science issued a White Paper that stated:

> The plans assume that expenditure will be reduced by one-third (about £15 million in a full academic year) below the 1978-79 level from September 1980 onwards. If most of this saving is achieved through increased fees, enrollments should not substantially fall below the current level of about 2 million students on evening and other courses [cited from "Commentary," 1980, p. 5].

It was clear that local authority adult education classes were to bear the brunt of these cuts, and the fees would have to rise substantially. Fears for adult education were such that at that time it appeared that some local authorities would just stop offering any form of service. Movement was afoot to take these local authorities to court on the basis of the 1944 act, which had never been tested in a court of law. However, this did not prove necessary.

Another indication of the fears for local authority general adult education at this time was the formation of a new pressure group—Save Adult Education Campaign—which perhaps indicates the fears that adult educators had at this time for the future of the service. Indeed, the Advisory Council for Adult and Continuing Education (ACACE) issued a report, *Protecting the Future for Adult Education,* in which it recognized the tremendous inroads into the service that the government cuts had made. Among its recommendations was one that stated:

> The Advisory Council considers that the present circumstances require the clear indication of a *minimum threshold commitment* to adult general education by which central government and the local education authorities may judge the adequacy of their policies and provision for the adult education service. The main aim must be to safeguard the present reduced level of provision. Any further reductions will disable the service and jeopardize its recovery [ACAE, 1981, p. 54].

This statement went on to specify the elements of the minimum threshold commitment about which it wanted discussion. It never occurred. Further cuts have occurred, and the Advisory Council has been disbanded by the government. The National Institute of Adult Education became the National Institute of Adult Continuing Education in 1984, following the demise of the Advisory Council, and it has assumed responsibility for some aspects of the government's policy of offering continuing education opportunities to the unemployed. Gradually, the institute has changed its role. This may not be wrong in any way at all, for had the institute not done so, then it would have undoubtedly been bypassed by the government and have been made to appear irrelevant to the latter's present policies.

Yet adult general education is extremely resilient. Many adult educators have worked far beyond the call of duty to ensure that it would survive, and so it has. Much more self-supporting, innovative, and, in many ways, more confident than ever before, a general adult education service is still offered throughout the land—a "poor cousin" of education generally but even more, a "poor cousin" of the vocational elements of continuing education itself.

This section has sought to demonstrate the problems experienced by the established service of general adult education over the past few years. It depicts what has happened to one element of continuing education within the United Kingdom in a short period of time and shows how government policy has divided one element of continuing education from another. It is now necessary to analyze the model of society on which these policies are based and to show how education is located within it.

An Analysis of the Place of Continuing Education Within Society

It may be seen from the whole of this volume that there has been a deliberate policy by the present government to direct continuing education along specific lines. Naturally, this is part of that government's responsibilities, and if they were not assumed, then the government would be guilty of negligence. However, it is important for educators to analyze the process and to highlight those significant issues that appear. In this book, it is clear that the government has adopted a certain policy toward education that assumes that, in some way, its main aim is to service certain dominant aspects of society, namely the needs of industry and commerce. Hence, those elements of continuing education that might be regarded as continuing vocational education have became more dominant and those that respond to the desires of individuals have become less dominant, unless those needs relate to employment in some way.

This does not mean that the government is financing all forms of continuing vocational education, as demonstrated in Chapter Seven. Neither does it mean that the government has deliberately set out to disband all adult general education but rather that those who desire to spend their time and money in this way might do so—but the government sees no reason why it should spend scarce resources on any individual's leisure time pursuits, however laudable those pursuits.

Certain priorities are clearly seen, and these relate to the financial and technological infrastructure of society. Indeed, Kerr and others (1973) argued as early as 1960, when their book was first published in the United States, that education is the handmaiden to industrialism. They specified that

> Industrialization requires an educational system functionally related to the skills and professions imperative to its technology. Such an educational system is not primarily concerned with conserving traditional values or perpetuating the classics. . . . The higher educational system of the industrial society stresses the natural sciences, engineering, medicine, managerial training—whether private or public—and administrative law. . . . The increased leisure time of industrialism, however, can afford a broader public appreciation of the arts [p. 47].

Here, then, is a basis for understanding the present government policies in the United Kingdom. While the quotation commences with the language of functionalism, the model of society that emerges is by no means a simplistic functional system. The model might be termed a neotechnological model, which places industry/technology as an infrastructure and all else, especially education, as part of the superstructure of society. As the shape of the infrastructure alters, the superstructure must adjust to meet its demands. Hence, education must always be the servant of industry and technology, and its curricula, whether they be in initial education or continuing education, must adjust to respond to those social pressures.

But, it might be asked, is society really structured in this manner? This is a fundamental question, because if this model of society is incorrect, it would present a basis from which to criticize the policy. However, there is no agreed-upon model of society within sociological analysis; thus, criticism of policy based on models of society can only be sustained if the model holds up to analysis. Certainly, there are other models that do not place quite such great emphasis on industrialism. Indeed, it is widely accepted that the model that Kerr and others (1973) produced of the industrialization process is overly simple and therefore not totally correct; so it might be argued that the policy of the present government is based on an overly simple set of premises.

Another way to criticize this approach is to indicate that the overemphasis on technology and vocationalism is even being questioned by those who are involved in professional education. Pelligrino (1977, p. 12), for instance, wishes to see the humanities included in the professional education curriculum, with respect to medicine. However, this approach does not command universal approval among those who are involved in vocational education. Thus, it is not as strong a critical position as the previous one.

However, it might also be asked whether this government's policies can be defended educationally. Clearly, there must be some rationale behind them, since they have been embraced so enthusiastically. It can be argued that governments have to make policy decisions and that these decisions must be practical within what is possible. Education is only one aspect of the wider set of policies that government is required to enact. Therefore, once it has been decided that only a certain sum of money should be spent on education, then priorities have to be decided, and action has to follow. If one accepts those priorities, then the outcome is logical, and the government has been consistent in the approach that is has adopted toward continuing education.

Looking to the Future

This chapter has described the manner in which continuing education has changed over the past decade in the United Kingdom. It has highlighted the fact that there has been a great increase in the emphasis on continuing vocational education and that there has been a considerable decline in support for adult general education. Clearly, these few years have changed the face of continuing education in this country for years to come. Is it, therefore, possible to predict the direction in which continuing education will develop within the next few years?

Prediction is always a difficult business, since society is not an impersonal system, and people are not cogs in machines. Yet there has always been some desire to predict, and humankind has made a habit of trying to deduce future events from present data. This is not a rigorous science; de Jouvenel (1967) called it "proference." He noted that there is no reason for assuming that there is an exact correspondence between the process of proference and the process of history. Yet the two may be drawn together, as the future is predicted from an analysis of present tendencies. The continuation of these present trends for continuing education depend on the manner in which the government enacts its policies based on its own ideological preferences and its understanding of the manner by which society functions. For as long as the government is consistent in this, it might be expected that the present pattern will continue.

However, it must be pointed out that this assertion is itself a denial of the model of society that sees technology as the infrastructure of society, since it is the demands of government rather than the demands of technology that perpetuate the present trends. If government was to change, or if government policy was to change, then the present trends might not continue. However, there are no signs that the latter might occur, and since the former may not happen within the next few years, there is every likelihood that continuing education will develop in the way that has been described thus far in this book.

References

Advisory Council on Adult and Continuing Education (ACACE). *Towards Continuing Education.* Leicester, UK: ACACE, 1979.
Advisory Council on Adult and Continuing Education (ACACE). *Protecting the Future of Adult Education.* Leicester, UK: ACACE, 1981.
"Commentary." *Adult Education,* 1980, 53 (1), 2-5.
de Jouvenal, B. *The Art of Conjecture.* London: Weidenfeld and Nicholson, 1967.
Kelly, T. *A History of Adult Education in Great Britain.* (2nd ed.) Liverpool, UK: Liverpool University Press, 1970.
Kerr, C., Dunlop, J. T., Harbison, E., and Myers, C. *Industrialism and Industrial Man.* (2nd ed.) Harmonsworth, UK: Pelican, 1973.
Pelligrino, E. D. "Report on the Conference of Professional Education." In B. A. Boley (ed.), *Crossfire in Professional Education.* New York: Pergamon, 1977.

Peter Jarvis is senior lecturer in the education of adults, University of Surrey, Guildford, Surrey, UK.

This chapter seeks to draw together some of the points raised in the preceding chapters that might have some relevance to the North American scene.

Some Implications for Continuing Education in North America

Peter Jarvis

The previous nine chapters have endeavored to depict some of the trends that are occurring in continuing education in the United Kingdom. It will have no doubt been noticed that some of these innovations, such as the Job Club, first occurred in North America, and, indeed, it is often claimed that much that happens in the United Kingdom occurs first in America. However, it will have been apparent from these accounts that this is not totally correct and that there are events in continuing education occurring in the United Kingdom that have not happened in the same way in America.

Comparison between the two countries might not be a totally valid exercise, since the countries have had different sociopolitical systems since World War II, as Chapter Two shows. However, Charters (1981) makes the point that one of the purposes of international comparative adult education is to help educators improve their own practice by having a more profound knowledge of adult education in general. If the provision of additional knowledge about continuing education in the United Kingdom can have that effect on any continuing educator in North America, then this volume will have exceeded the authors' expectations. Indeed, it is hoped that the book has presented some analyses that help to shed new perspectives on the current trends in education. The purpose of this chapter, therefore, is to try to underline a few of these points, without seeking in any way to suggest that what is occurring in the United Kingdom is unique or different from anything occurring in the United States.

Policy Analyses

Chapter Two of this book seeks to show how the education of adults can be analyzed from the perspective of government welfare policy. This insightful approach highlights the manner by which the education of adults is being segmented into different forms and how some are receiving more government support than others. Indeed, it also shows how education is responsive to the economic infrastructure of society. A similar theme is echoed in Chapter Nine, where the future of liberal adult education is discussed. This division between adult and continuing education is one that may be witnessed in many North American universities, with their departments of adult education and the centers for continuing education. It might be claimed that the former is about the academic study and the latter about the provision of the education of adults and that the two work in harmony, as they most certainly do. But are they really about the same form of education? Is the analysis for the United Kingdom valid for America? The American Association of Adult and Continuing Education has sought to bring together the two forms within its title, and this is most commendable. But the question must be asked as to whether there are two totally different forms of the education of adults within that title and whether there are different policy decisions about them. Indeed, even more basic questions do need to be asked about whether there is a difference between the two forms of education in America and, if there is, whether it actually matters.

Certainly, there is both federal and state policy about adult and continuing education, and there has also been an effective lobby over the years for the education of adults in America. The greater the knowledge about the trends that are occurring within this field, the more effective the lobby can be.

Adult Learning and Continuing Education

The above analysis might be taken a little further, for it is common to hear adult educators in both countries talk of individual needs, and one of the effects of adult education is to produce change agents. But if continuing education is a response to industrial and technological change, then it might merely be helping people to adapt to change and to conform to the expectations created by the changed social conditions. If this analysis is true, then adult educators have confused individual needs with social needs, and the resulting conformity is the end of education. The change agent has been confused with the changed person who has learned to adapt and the education of adults regarded as intrinsically good because it has supported the social change.

Such an analysis calls into question the vocabulary and, perhaps, also the myths of adult education. Need is seen as individualistic, because much of the study of adult learning is individual and necessarily psychological. However, continuing education is a social institution, and its study necessarily sociological. Learning produces change in behavior, so that it is easy to see how the myth of the changed person originates—even if the social outcome of the learning is a change in the direction of society's expectations of conformity. This is not to claim that the original connotations are necessarily entirely wrong, only that they have limited validity and that their usage needs some reconsideration.

Education and the Wider Society

A consistent theme running through this volume has been the manner in which there is an interrelationship between the education of adults and the wider society. Thus, these analyses have constantly referred to the unemployment crisis, the decline in the membership of labor unions, government policy, and so on. In addition, the studies have shown the breadth of adult education provision in that wider society. Most important, some of the crises in society have produced significant educational innovations. Clearly, these things are also happening in America, where there are a great number of very significant and exciting innovations in the education such as the work at Wayne State University with the unemployed, the work of the Highlander Center with labor unions, and some of the exciting educational programs with the underprivileged. Hence, these studies are presented here as examples of what is happening in the United Kingdom in continuing education at a time of rapid social and economic change.

Open Learning and Access

One of the most significant things that present government policy has created within the educational system in the United Kingdom has been the realization that the system has to adapt to change. It might be argued that the government has pushed this policy much too far and that it has mistakenly sought to treat educational institutions in precisely the same manner as factories and other organizations of material production. Yet the policy has created change. Educational institutions have responded to that change, and they have become more open to the wider society and its needs. This has produced curricular change of significant proportions, as Chapter Eight on open learning suggests. Open learning itself has become a crucial concept within the education vocabulary. Not all the changes have been commendable, but wider access to education, offering educational guidance to those who are not sure of what to study next, flexibility in study arrangements, and more adults able to enjoy the privilege of formalized learning have been beneficial outcomes. Educational institutions offering courses on the open market, advertising their wares, and even, perhaps, creating learning needs in people through this advertising is much less commendable. Both can occur within the present climate, and it is easy to slip from support and service to selling education as a commodity in order to survive. This is perhaps nothing new to practitioners of other professions, but it is a new situation for adult educators. It is one that occurs in the development of all the people professions, and it is perhaps to them that adult educators have to look for some of the solutions to these problems.

Education and the People

Space prevented a full discussion of all aspects of continuing education in the United Kingdom, and there is, for instance, little mention in this volume of community education, although the community program initiated by the Manpower Services Commission has been mentioned. Yet other aspects of education and the underprivileged and the working classes, the labor unions, and the unemployed have been discussed. It is easy, especially at a time when resources are restricted, to concentrate only on the most privileged aspects of society. It is easier to study continuing professional education than it is education and the labor unions, easier to study education and the work place than it is education and the unemployed, easier to study education and the professions than it is education and blue-collar workers, easier to study liberal adult education and the middle classes than it is education and the working classes. Yet students of continuing education in all societies have to be wary that they do not fall into the trap of studying what society deems the more important and successful and thereby merely unthinkingly reproducing its dominant values. The study of continuing education is indeed a broad field containing many specializations, and disservice is done to its richness if its breadth is not included within either its research purview or its curriculum.

Education and the Professions

One of the contrasts in this volume has been the way in which Todd and Piper (Chapters Three and Four) have concentrated on change within the educational institutions, while Welsh (Chapter Seven) studied professional education within the professions themselves. Educators within the traditional educational institutions have considered education their prerogative for a long time—perhaps too long. It is important that educational institutions adapt in order to accommodate aspects of development of continuing education, but there is a danger in "throwing the baby out with the bathwater." All that went before was not bad, and educational institutions have to retain the good as they dispense with what is no longer of academic value. However, they should not expect to retain their monopoly of provision. This is implicit in Chapter Seven and explicit in other writings, such as Eurich's (1985) excellent study in the United States. In this way, the United Kingdom seems to be following the lead set in the United States, with both the professions and employers developing their own courses of study within their own educational institutions and awarding credit for the study successfully undertaken.

Conclusions

This chapter has sought to draw together some of the issues that have been implicit in this volume and to raise some questions about them. The questions have been valid for both societies rather than just for North American adult education, although it is hoped that North American adult educators will feel that the issues are relevant to their practice.

Continuing education is a complex phenomenon (Jarvis, 1986) that is rapidly undergoing change. Much of its complexity has necessarily been omitted, and some of what is recorded may be out of date by the time this volume is published. However, it is anticipated that the issues discussed in this final chapter will retain their validity somewhat longer.

References

Charters, A. N., and Associates. *Comparing Adult Education Worldwide.* San Francisco: Jossey Bass, 1981.
Eurich, N. *Corporate Classrooms.* Princeton, N.J.: Carnegie Foundation for the Advancement of Teaching, 1985.
Jarvis, P. *Sociological Analysis of Lifelong Education and Lifelong Learning.* Department of Adult Education, Athens: University of Georgia, 1986.

Peter Jarvis is senior lecturer in the education of adults at the University of Surrey, Guildford, Surrey, UK.

Index

A

Access, in higher education 30-31, 41, 78, 79, 96
Access Centers, 39
Accredited Training Centers, 42-43
Action for Jobs Program, 59
Adult education, 1-2, 24, 26-27, 50, 55-56; and continuing education, 3-7, 28, 30, 94; government policy and, 5, 6, 14-21, 52
Adult education centers, 9, 33, 40-42
Adult Education Committee (AEC), 14, 18
Adult Training Schemes, 38
Adult Training Strategy, 28, 38, 39
Advisory Council for Adult and Continuing Education (ACACE), 4, 10, 18-22, 85, 88, 91
Agricultural studies, 27
American Association of Adult and Continuing Education, 94
Ancient history, 26
Anderson, D., 54
Apprenticeships, 36, 37
Approved training organization status, 42
Archaeology, 26
Armstrong, P. F., 20, 22

B

Bagley, B., 79, 82
Bargaining Information, 49
Bartlett School of Architecture, 71
Barnet College of Further Education, 78, 82
Bates, A., 81, 82
Berryman, 61, 62
Beveridge, Lord, 55, 62
Bilham, T., 28, 32
Binary system of higher education, 24-25, 28
Biology, 26
Birch, D., 81, 82
Birkbeck College, 7

Boley, B. A., 91
Bridging courses, 50
British Department of Education and Science (DES), 32, 33, 35-37, 42, 44; higher education and, 8, 26, 27-29, 39-40, 65; open learning and, 80, 81, 86-87; vocational education, 6, 57, 59-60
British Department of Employment, 28, 35, 36, 56, 57, 59
British Department of Health and Social Security, 57
British Department of Trade and Industry, 6, 40
British Ministry of Reconstruction, 14
Burgess, T., 23, 32
Business skills, 10, 37, 39, 41, 58-59

C

Capitalism, 14, 16, 18, 19-20
Careers Service, 58
CEM, 70
Challis, B., 79, 82
Charnley, A. H., 57, 62
Chartered Society of Physiotherapists, 71
Charters, A. N., 93, 97
Childcare, 51
Church of Rome, 9
Churches, 8, 9, 14, 60
Citizens advice bureaus, 60
Code of Practice, 48
Colleges of further education, 33-44, 59; government policy and, 6-7, 27; trade unions and, 47, 48, 49, 51
Colleges of higher education 5-6, 24, 31, 39, 56, 80
"Commentary," 87, 91
Commerce, 2, 9, 60, 89
Commercial training, 9, 35, 80
Commission on Industrial Relations (CIR), 47-48, 54
Community colleges (U.K.), 5, 7
Community colleges (U.S.), 7

99

Community Program, 38-39, 43, 59
Competence, standards of, 66-69, 71
Computing studies, 26, 41
Conference centers, 9
Conservative administration, 20, 21, 89; social policy of, 13-14, 16, 23; trade unions and, 46, 47, 49, 53
Conset, 59
Construction Group, 66, 73
Construction Industry Training Board, 71
Construction professions, 66, 71
Continuing education, definition of, 3-7, 18-19, 28, 29-30, 94
Continuing education and training (CET), 66
Continuing professional development (CPD), 66-67
Cooperative Development Association, 59
Correspondence colleges, 9
Costello, N., 19, 22
Council for National Academic Awards (CNAA), 9, 24, 30, 32, 42
Credit Accumulation and Transfer Scheme (CATS), 9, 30-31, 41
Creigh, S., 54

D

Davies, D., 78, 82
Davies, M., 57, 62
Day-release courses, 47, 48, 49, 50
de Jouvenel, B., 91
Delphy, C., 20, 22
Denmark, 8
Development Council for Adult Education, 3-4
Disabled workers, 51
Disadvantaged adults, 8, 95
Distance learning, 7, 39, 52; open learning and, 76, 77; professional education and, 69, 70
Drake, K., 21, 22
Duke, C., 28, 32
Duke, F., 31, 32
Dunlop, J. T., 89, 90, 91

E

Economic policy, 33, 49, 53; adult education and, 18, 23, 31, 94; social welfare and, 20, 21; trade unions and, 45, 46
Education, studies in, 26
Education Act (1944), 5, 33, 86, 87
Education Support Grants, 57
Educational Advice Grants, 58
Educational technology, 76
Elton, L., 81, 82
Employment and Enterprise Group, 38
Employment Protection Act (1975), 48
Employment training, 43
Employment Training Act, (1973), 35
Engineering, 26, 27, 66
Engineering Council, 69
England, 3, 4-9, 39, 78
Enterprise Allowance Scheme, 38-39, 58
Entwistle, J., 30, 32
Equality of opportunity, principle of, 19, 36
Ethnic minorities, 51, 60
Eurich, N., 97
European Bureau of Adult Education, 61
Evans, N., 30, 32
Examinations, 33-34, 37, 39, 41, 66
Experiential learning, 30, 31, 76
Exports training, center for, 28, 31
Extension courses, 26
External degree programs, 7, 25-26
Extramural courses, 7, 24, 26, 28, 85-87; trade unions and, 47, 48, 49

F

Fabian socialism, 14
Finch, G., 16, 22
Fisher, H., 57, 62
Flexistudy, 78, 79
France, 61
Freeman, R., 78, 82
Friedman, M., 16, 17
Functional adaptation and integration, policy model of, 21
Functionalism, 89
Further education, 1, 66, 78, 79; government policy and, 4-5, 10, 86; unemployment and, 56, 59. *See also* Colleges of further education
Further Education Unit, 65, 81, 82

G

General Certificate of Education, 6
George, V., 14, 22
Germany, 61
Griffin, C., 13-22
Grugeon, D., 77, 83

H

Handy, C., 58, 62
Harbison, E., 89, 90, 91
Heiner, M., 61, 62
Higher education, 1, 8-9, 56, 66; government policy and, 5, 10, 19, 43; open learning and, 41-42, 78-80. *See also* Colleges of higher education
Highlander Center, 95
Hillcroft College, 8
History, studies in, 26
Hobrough, J., 61, 62
Holford, J., 2, 45-54
Houle, C., 70, 73

I

Incorporated Society of Valuers and Auctioneers (ISVA), 70, 72
Independent study, 31, 70, 76, 77, 78
Industrial performance-achievement model, 18
Industrial Revolution, 34
Industrial skills, studies in, 37
Industrial Training Act (1964), 34-35
Industrialism, 89-90
Industry, 8, 9, 10, 34-35, 45-54, 80; educational collaboration with, 2, 23, 28, 31, 38-40, 43, 60; as educational priority, 20, 89-90, 94
Inflation, 46, 55
Institution of Structural Engineers, 71
Introductory Course for Union Representatives, 48, 49

J

Jarvis, P., 1-11, 15, 22, 85-97
Job Centers, 57
Job Clubs, 58, 93
Job exchanges, 70
Job-finding skills, 58
Job Training Program, 35, 37, 59-60
Joint training, 54
Jones, B., 26, 27, 32

K

Kelly, T. A., 85, 91
Kerr, T., 89, 90, 91
Knowles, M. S., 3, 10

L

Labor administration, 14, 46, 48
Labor unions, 10, 95, 96. *See also* Trade unions
Lancashire Polytechnic, 78
Language studies, 9, 26, 28
Latham, J., 81, 82
Law, 26, 66
Law Society, 69, 70
Lawton, E., 61, 62
Leisure courses, 1-2, 9, 24, 41, 56; government policy and, 4, 5, 89
Leonard, P., 20, 22
Levy/grant system, 35
Lewis, R., 75, 76, 82
Liberal adult education, 24, 26-27; continuing education and, 28, 30, 94; government policy and, 5, 6, 14-21
Liberg-progressive model, of social welfare policy, 14, 15, 16-20
Liberalism, 14, 53
Literature, study of, 26
Liverpool Riverside constituency, 56
Local employers' networks, 38
Lucas, S., 78, 82, 83

M

MacDonald, J., 57, 62
McIlroy, J., 49, 54
MacIntosh, N., 4, 10
MacKenzie, N., 76, 83
Management studies, 26, 27, 37, 39
Manpower Services Commission (MSC), 20, 44, 83; further education and, 6, 33, 42; government policy and, 19, 35-40, 43; higher education and, 21, 27-28, 31; open learning and, 71, 80, 96; unemployment and, 57, 58; vocational education and, 59, 79

Mansbridge, A., 8
Market model, of social welfare policy, 15-16
Marxism, 19-20
Mathematics, 26
Medical studies, 26-90
Midwives, 69
Mobile training services, 39
Morris, H., 7
Music studies, 26
Myers, C., 89, 90, 91

N

National Advisory Body for Local Authority Higher Education (NABLAHE), 25, 27, 32
National Advisory Body for Public Sector Higher Education, 41-42
National Council for Adult and Continuing Education, 4
National Council for Vocational Qualifications (NCVQ), 34, 44
National Extension College (NEC), 78, 79, 80, 83
National Institute of Adult Continuing Education, 61, 88
National Institute of Adult Education, 88
National Training Initiative, 79
Nationalization, 14
Neotechnological model, of society, 89-90, 91
New Job Training Scheme, 37-38
"New Training Initiative," 36-37
New Training Initiative: An Agenda for Action, 36-37, 44
NEXUS, 61
North America, 1, 7, 89, 93-97
North East London Polytechnic, 78
North of England Council for Providing Higher Education for Women, 7
Northern College, 8
Northern Ireland, 8
North/South Divided Nation Debate, 56

O

Off-the-job training, 39, 59
Office of Population Censuses and Surveys (OPCS), 34, 44

Oil crisis, 55
On-the-job training, 30, 36, 37, 70
Open Business School, 80
Open College, 38, 80, 83
Open College of the North West (OCNW), 78
Open colleges movement, 78-79
Open learning, 75-82, 96
Open Learning Unit, 79
Open School, 52
Open Tech program, 36, 38, 79, 80, 81
Open University, 2, 6, 7, 22, 25; government policy and, 4, 18; open learning and, 76-77, 78, 80, 81
Overborrowing, public sector, 55

P

Part-time provision, 7, 25-26, 28, 56; open access through, 8, 24, 30, 79
Pelligrino, E. D., 90, 91
Percy, K., 78, 83
Perry, W., 77, 83
Phillipson, C., 20, 22
Physical science, studies in, 26
Physiotherapists, 69
PICKUP program, 27-29, 39-40, 65; open learning and, 80, 81; unemployment and, 57, 60
Pinker, R., 14, 22
Piper, L. S., 1, 33-44, 96-97
Plater College, 9
Polytechnics, 1, 23-31, 33, 56; collaboration in, 7-8, 9, 38, 39-40, 49; continuing education and, 5-6, 19, 87; open access to, 41, 80
Postal course model, 52
Postcompulsory eduation, 1, 3, 33, 39, 43-44
Postgate, R., 76, 83
Postqualifying legal education (PQLE), 66
Preston Polytechnic, 78
Privatization, 43
Proference, 91
Professional education, 33-34, 56, 65-73, 97; collaboration in, 8, 9, 24, 60, 80
"Professional Studies in British Architectural Practice," 71-72

Protecting the Future for Adult Education, 88, 91
Pump-priming, 8, 79, 80, 86

Q

Qualifications, formal, 9, 34, 35, 37-38, 40-41, 42

R

Racism, 51, 60
Recession, 55
Recreative learning, 15, 17, 41. *See also* Leisure
Redistribution of life changes, principle of, 19
Redistributive state interference, principle of, 16
Religion, 8, 9, 14, 60
REPLAN, 57, 61
Research funding, 25
Residential colleges, 8-9
Residential folk high schools, 8
Residual welfare model, of social welfare policy, 15
Responsible body status, 7, 8, 26, 28, 86, 87
RESTART, 58
Review of Vocational Qualifications, 33-34
Richardson, M., 19, 22
Rights at Work, Health and Safety at Work, 49
Robbins, Lord, 24, 25, 32
Robbins Committee, 24
Robertson, D., 78, 82
Royal Commission on Trade Unions and Employers Associations, 46, 53, 54
Royal Institute of British Architects (RIBA), 70, 71-72
Royal Institution of Chartered Surveyors, 70, 72
Royal Town Planning Institute (RTPI), 67, 71, 72-73
Rumble, G., 81, 83
Ruskin College, 8
Russell, L., 3-4, 8, 10, 17, 22
Russell Report, 3-4, 8, 17-19, 20

S

Sacks, H., 78, 83
Safety representatives, 48, 49
Sarup, M., 22
Save Adult Education Campaign 88
Scotland, 4, 8, 39
Scottish Education Department, 79, 83
Scupham, J., 76, 83
Self-employment, 58
Self-financing courses, 28
Self-help groups, 60
Shop stewards, 46-51, 53
Skillcenters, 39
Skills competency, tests for, 37
Skills Training Agency, 39
Small businesses, 38, 41, 58-59
Smith, A., 16, 17
Smith, G., 57, 62
Social control model, of social welfare policy, 15, 18-21
Social welfare policy, 13-21, 94
Socialism, 14, 53
Society of Friends, 9
Sociology, studies in, 26
Spencer, D., 75, 79, 82, 83
Staff development, 42-43, 61, 68
Stephenson, J., 78, 83
Stock, A., 5, 10, 91
Storrie, T., 59, 62
Stuart, J., 7, 85
Student-centered learning, 46, 52
Study groups, 52
Styler, W., 15, 22
Supervisory skills, studies in, 37, 39
Systematic home reading, 70

T

"Tackling Racism," 51
Tawney, R., 17, 22
Taxation, local, 15
Taylor, D., 56, 62
Teacher training colleges, 5
Technical and Vocational Education Initiative, 31
Technology, 89-90, 91, 94
Technology, studies in, 26, 27, 39, 56
Technology transfer, centers for, 28, 31
Technophobia, 59

Thatcher, M., 13, 15, 16, 21
Thorpe, M., 77, 83
Tight, M., 2, 25, 32, 75-83
Titmus, 19, 22
Titmuss, 14, 18, 22
Todd, F., 1, 23-32, 96-97
Toombs, F., 54
Town and country planning, studies in, 26
Townswomen's Guild, 8
Trade Union Studies Centers, 49
Trade unions, 2, 45-54, 60, 86. *See also* Labor unions
Trades Union Congress (TUC), 45-54
TUC Training College, 48-49
TUC Workbook on Racism, 51
Training Commission, 6, 31, 57
Training for Employment, 43, 44
"Training for the Future," 35
Training Opportunities Scheme, 35, 37, 38
Training Shop Stewards, 46, 54
Turner, M., 59, 62
Tutors, 48, 49, 51, 52, 60, 61

U

Underprivileged adults, 8, 95
Unemployed adults, 38-39, 95, 96; government policy and, 15, 49, 88; training for, 10, 35, 37, 55-62
Unified Vocational Preparation Scheme, 35, 36
United States, 1, 7, 89, 93-97
Universities, 2, 23-31, 33, 85-87, 94; collaboration in, 7-8, 9, 38, 39-40; higher education and, 1, 5-6, 19, 56; open access to, 41, 80; trade unions and, 47, 48, 49
University of Cambridge, 7
University extension movement, 7
University Grants Commission (UGC), 4, 10, 32; government policy through, 24, 25, 27; open access and, 41, 86
University of Lancaster, 78
University of London, 7, 26
University of London External Degree System, 77, 78
University of Surrey, 7, 58

V

Venables, P., 4, 10
Venables Report, 4, 10
Visual arts, studies in, 26
Vocational education, 5, 67, 86, 89-90; adult education vs., 6, 26, 28, 30, 41, 85; government policy and, 19, 79-80, 82; unemployment and, 56, 59
Vocational Education and Training Group, 38

W

Wage drift, 46
Wales, 3, 4-9, 39
Waller, R., 14, 11, 22
Walters, N., 1, 55-63
Ward, P., 78, 82
Watts, A., 58, 62
Wayne State University, 95
Welfare capitalism, 14, 16, 19-20
Welfare state, 13-17
Welsh, L., 65-73, 97
Westwood, S., 7, 11
Wider Opportunities Training Program, 37
Wilding, P., 14, 22
Wilson, P., 30, 32
"Women and Health at Work," 50
"Women and Pensions," 50
Women Returners, 58
"Women and Sexual Harassment at Work," 50
Women's education, 7, 8, 15; work and, 37, 50-51, 58, 60
Women's Institute, 8
Woodbrooke College, 9
Work Study, Productivity, and Pay, 49
Workers' cooperatives, 59
Workers' Education Association (WEA), 8, 60, 86; trade unions and, 2, 10, 47, 48, 49, 51
Working Party Report, 46

Y

Young, Lord, 23, 32
Youth Opportunities Program, 35, 36
Youth Training Scheme, 35, 36, 37, 42-43

STATEMENT OF OWNERSHIP, MANAGEMENT AND CIRCULATION

1A. Title of Publication	1B. PUBLICATION NO.	2. Date of Filing
New Directions for Continuing Education	4 9 3 - 9 3 0	10/26/88

3. Frequency of Issue	3A. No. of Issues Published Annually	3B. Annual Subscription Price
quarterly	4	$39 indiv./ $52 inst.

4. Complete Mailing Address of Known Office of Publication:
350 Sansome Street, San Francisco, CA 94104

5. Complete Mailing Address of the Headquarters of General Business Offices of the Publisher:
350 Sansome Street, San Francisco, CA 94104

6. Full Names and Complete Mailing Address of Publisher, Editor, and Managing Editor:
Publisher: Jossey-Bass Inc., Publishers, 350 Sansome Street, San Francisco, CA 94109
Editor: Gordon Darkenwald, Graduate School of Education, Rutgers University, 10 Seminary Pl., New Brunswick, NJ 08903
Managing Editor: Allen Jossey-Bass, Jossey-Bass Inc., Publishers, 350 Sansome Street, San Francisco, CA 94104

7. Owner:

Full Name	Complete Mailing Address
Jossey-Bass Inc., Publishers	350 Sansome Street, San Francisco, CA 94104

For names and addresses of stockholders, see attached list

8. Known Bondholders, Mortgagees, and Other Security Holders Owning or Holding 1 Percent or More of Total Amount of Bonds, Mortgages or Other Securities:

Full Name	Complete Mailing Address
same as #7	

10. Extent and Nature of Circulation:

	Average No. Copies Each Issue During Preceding 12 Months	Actual No. Copies of Single Issue Published Nearest to Filing Date
A. Total No. Copies	1400	1491
B. Paid and/or Requested Circulation		
1. Sales through dealers and carriers, street vendors and counter sales	149	10
2. Mail Subscription	614	620
C. Total Paid and/or Requested Circulation	763	630
D. Free Distribution by Mail, Carrier or Other Means, Samples, Complimentary, and Other Free Copies	144	210
E. Total Distribution	907	840
F. Copies Not Distributed		
1. Office use, left over, unaccounted, spoiled after printing	493	651
2. Return from News Agents		
G. TOTAL	1400	1491

11. I certify that the statements made by me above are correct and complete

Signature and Title of Editor, Publisher, Business Manager, or Owner: Vice-President

PS Form 3526, Dec. 1987